The Christian's Everyday Problems

The Christian's Everyday Problems

By
Leroy Brownlow

BROWNLOW PUBLISHING COMPANY, INC.
FORT WORTH, TEXAS

Copyright 1966

Brownlow Publishing Company, Inc.
6309 Airport Freeway, Fort Worth, Texas 76117

Contents

CHAPTER		PAGE
	FOREWORD	5
I.	THE PROBLEM OF ABUNDANT LIVING	9
II.	THE PROBLEM OF DISCERNMENT	18
III.	THE PROBLEM OF IMMATURITY	27
IV.	THE PROBLEM OF WORRY	35
V.	THE PROBLEM OF ENEMIES	44
VI.	THE PROBLEM OF FRIENDS	53
VII.	THE PROBLEM OF TIME	62
VIII.	THE PROBLEM OF EMPLOYMENT	71
IX.	THE PROBLEM OF INDIVIDUAL LEADERSHIP	80
X.	THE PROBLEM OF CONTRARY WINDS	90
XI.	THE PROBLEM OF SELF-IMPRISONMENT	99
XII.	THE PROBLEM OF SELF-DISCOVERY	108
XIII.	THE PROBLEM OF SELF-IMPROVEMENT	118

Foreword

THIS book, THE CHRISTIAN'S EVERYDAY PROBLEMS, is what the title suggests: a discussion of our daily problems and their solutions. It would be a hopeless task to try to specify and study all the problems of life; so in this volume we have considered only some of the major and basic ones, together with certain principles which can strengthen us for all circumstances.

"Man that is born of a woman is of few days, and full of trouble" (Job 14:1) — so he has his problems. This has been true since the downfall of the race in the early dawn of time. Through the centuries man has had to struggle in a world of thorns and thistles (Gen. 3:17,18). The Christian is no exception; he has his problems, too, even though they are fewer and less difficult to handle because of his life of faith, hope and love.

It has been "my heart's desire and prayer to God" to make available in this book a series of practical lessons dealing with man's needs seven days a week. There are many studies on the church, worship, the Bible and doctrinal matters, but there is a scarcity of studies designed to give strength for daily problems. Aware of the growing pressures and complications of life, we have felt it very timely to present to the Bible-studying public this series of studies.

These lessons were designed for all Bible classes of men, women, and young people beginning with high school.

With the consciousness of the responsibility resting upon an author and with another prayer unto God, we now send this volume on its mission, entertaining the hope that it may give direction, inspiration and power for the perplexing situations which try us daily.

LEROY BROWNLOW

Fort Worth, Texas
U. S. A.

I
The Problem of Abundant Living

I. INTRODUCTION

SCIENCE has been able to add years to life, but the greatest problem is how to add life to years. Abundant living is an art and we should apply ourselves to the earthly duty of cultivating it.

1. *The art of living is not necessarily found in many years of existence.* Methuselah lived 969 years (Gen. 5:27); but, so far as we know, he never accomplished one worthwhile thing.

> We live in deeds, not years; in thoughts, not breaths;
> In feelings, not figures on a dial.
> We should count time by heart throbs: He most lives
> Who thinks most, feels the noblest, acts the best.

2. *Successful living is not incumbent on secular knowledge.* Solomon was the wisest man of all ages; yet he exclaimed, "For in much wisdom is much grief: and he that increaseth knowledge increaseth sorrow" (Eccl. 1:18). A knowledge which forgets God leads to sorrow.

3. *Neither is graceful living achieved in the accumulation of wealth.* Jesus said, "A man's life consisteth not in the abundance of the things which he possesseth" (Lk. 12:15). One may effect financial success and be unhappy, miserable and die a failure.

II. BOUNTEOUS LIVING REVOLVES AROUND A GREAT CENTER

1. An illustrative story was told by Admiral Byrd con-

cerning his first expedition to the South Pole. He said that he left his isolated hut one day for a brief trip of exploration, and then in a sudden blizzard he became hopelessly lost. In that barren whiteness there was nothing to give him any sense of direction. He knew if he should strike out blindly to find his hut, and if he should fail, the chances are he would freeze in the storm. He had a long pole which he always carried to feel for holes in the ice; so he stuck it in the snow and tied a scarf to it. He said: "That was my center. If I failed to find my hut, I could return to the center and try again. Three times I tried and failed; but each time I returned to my center, without which I would have been lost and would have died. In the fourth attempt, I stumbled upon my hut."

2. *Every life, to be safe, must have a center, a point of reference.* There must be a home port, a place where we can return. In mathematics it is found in the decimal point. In literature it is found in the basic rules of grammar. In religion it is found in Christ. "For to me to live is Christ" (Phil. 1:21). He is "the way, the truth, and the life" (Jno. 14:6).

3. *"To err is human."* We make mistakes. "If we say that we have no sin, we deceive ourselves, and the truth is not in us" (I Jno. 1:8). But as long as we have Jesus as our center and return to him for pardon, strength and direction, there is hope for us.

III. ABUNDANT LIVING REQUIRES OPTIMISM

1. *A pessimist says,* "If I don't try, I can't fail." *The optimist says,* "If I don't try, I can't win." It is the difference in the attitudes which makes for success for one and failure for the other. Optimism is one of the necessary qualities of success.

2. *A Christian should be exceedingly optimistic.* Paul tells us this and tells us why:

THE PROBLEM OF ABUNDANT LIVING

(1) "I can do all things through Christ which strengtheneth me" (Phil. 4:13) — through Christ.

(2) "If God be for us, who can be against us?" (Rom. 8:31) — God for us.

(3) "I will fear no evil: for thou art with me" (Psa. 23:4) — God with us.

(4) "Let not your heart be troubled: ye believe in God, believe also in me" (Jno. 14:1) — faith in God.

3. *Optimism gives one a sparkle and a magnetic attraction that pulls the world to him.* The world is not going to follow the man who has a gloomy outlook. We like the person who enjoys the doughnut rather than gripes at the hole in it. Many persons live in contemplation of their own troubles and dwell in their own expected defeats until they become imprisoned in disagreeableness and morbidity.

IV. THE ATTRACTIVE LIFE IS HESITANT TO FIND FAULT AND CRITICIZE

1. The meek and humble person has a consciousness of his own imperfections, which makes him *more tolerant of the faults of others.* Jesus said, "And why beholdest thou the mote that is in thy brother's eye, but considerest not the beam that is in thine own eye" (Matt. 7:3).

2. *The fault-finder condemns himself through his criticisms of others.* "For wherein thou judgest another, thou condemnest thyself; for thou that judgest doest the same things" (Rom. 2:1). The critic often starts false rumors on another in a futile effort to whitewash himself in his own sins. It makes him feel bigger and cleaner, but what a price he pays: condemns himself, lowers himself, kills friendships and repels the best of people . . . and just to try to make a little person feel big.

3. *We should not be discouraged when people find fault*

with us; for the only sinless one in this world had more critics than anyone — Jesus Christ. There are some people who, if they should go to heaven, would find fault with the golden street, the pearly gate and even complain that their halo was a misfit — if they should go there.

4. *We cannot please everybody;* but we can do right, and in the long run this is the only thing that really matters anyway; so let them criticize, if they will. "For it is better if the will of God be so, that ye suffer for well doing, than for evil doing" (I Pet. 3:17).

V. IT MAKES FOR NOBLER LIVING IF WE LEARN THAT THE OTHER FELLOW HAS HIS VIEWPOINT

1. *The view for every person is determined by the eyes doing the looking.* The Chinese delegate to the United Nations was besieged by reporters when he arrived in New York. One of the newspapermen asked, "What strikes you as one of the oddest things about Americans?" After a moment's hesitation, he said, "The peculiar slant of their eyes."

2. *Learning this lesson will help us to live easier and better with others.* It makes for peace, which is one of our everyday problems of living. "Let us therefore follow after the things which make for peace, and things wherewith one may edify another" (Rom. 14:19).

3. *Of course, God sanctions no person's following his own will to the neglect or perversion of God's will.* Jesus prayed, "Not as I will, but as thou wilt" (Matt. 26:39). He taught us to pray, "Thy will be done on earth, as it is in heaven" (Matt. 6:10).

VI. THE RICHER LIFE REQUIRES THAT WE BE ABLE TO ADMIT THAT WE HAVE BEEN WRONG

1. *Saying that you have been wrong about something*

should not be difficult, for it is the same as saying that you are wiser today than you were yesterday.

2. *The greatest and best people have made mistakes —* all because they were human.

(1) Moses believed not to sanctify the Lord in the eyes of Israel (Num. 20:10).

(2) Saul who spared the best sheep and oxen later said, "I have sinned" (I Sam. 15:24).

(3) Peter denied the Lord (Matt. 26:69-75).

(4) Saul made havoc of the church (Acts 8:3), and later admitted that he "did it ignorantly in unbelief" (I Tim. 1:13).

3. *The admission of guilt, sin, is a necessary quality of the Christian life.* We must confess to both God and man: (1) Confess to God — "Forgive us our debts, as we forgive our debtors" (Matt. 6:12). (2) Confess to man — "Confess your faults one to another, and pray one for another" (Jas. 5:16). We must not be like the poor deceived soul who said, "I think I would confess my mistakes, if I ever made any."

4. *We may try to avoid mistakes by doing nothing,* but that is the greatest mistake of all. "Therefore to him that knoweth to do good, and doeth it not, to him it is sin" (Jas. 4:17).

> He made no mistakes —
> Took no wrong road,
> He never fumbled the ball.
> He never went down
> 'Neath the weight of a load.
> He simply did nothing at all.

VII. FORGIVENESS IS A PREREQUISITE TO THE ABUNDANT LIFE

1. *Forgiveness is a beautiful act —* too beautiful for ugly

people; *a big thing* — too big for little people. It is the scent that flowers give when they are trampled on.

> Never does the human soul appear so strong as when it foregoes revenge, and dares to forgive an injury.
> — Chapin

2. *Forgiveness is one thing we cannot receive unless we are willing to give it to others.* "Forbearing one another, and forgiving one another, if any man have a quarrel against any: even as Christ forgave you, so also do ye" (Col. 3:13) — as Christ forgave you. "But if ye forgive not men their trespasses, neither will your father forgive your trespasses" (Matt. 6:15) — but man acts as if it were not so.

3. *Forgetfulness is one of the characteristics of true forgiveness.* This is the way God forgives, for it is pure and true — no make believe — and he remembers it no more. "And their sins and iniquities will I remember no more" (Heb. 10:17).

When the missionaries first went to Labrador they found no word for forgiveness in the Eskimo language. So they had to make a new word which in Eskimo literally meant "not-being-able-to-think-about-it-any-more."

Forgiveness which forgets enables one to put behind him all wrongs he has suffered from others and thus find a new life. This was true of Joseph who suffered the meanest treacheries and cruelist injustices at the hands of envious brothers who sold him into slavery. They sold only his body — they could not sell his spirit. With a free spirit and with God on his side, he climbed to the top. He knew that life is too wonderful to be ruined with hate and bitterness. In keeping with his disposition, "Joseph called the name of the firstborn Manasseh: For God, said he, hath made me forget all my toil, and all my father's house"

(Gen. 41:51). Thus it is noteworthy that we never read of Joseph's saying: "I resent . . ."; "I'm offended . . ."; "I've taken exception . . ."; "I don't like . . ."; "I've been mistreated . . ."; "I'm unhappy about . . ."; "I've forgiven but not forgotten . . ."; "I'll get even . . ." Joseph found the abundant life in forgiveness and forgetfulness; and it can never be found apart from this Christ-like bigness of heart.

4. *Forgiveness is a matter of mercy rather than justice.* A mother who knew this sought the pardon of her son from Napoleon. The emperor said it was his second offense, and justice demanded his death. The mother replied, "I don't ask for justice; I plead for mercy." "But," said the emperor, "he does not deserve mercy." The mother cried, "Sir, it would not be mercy, if he deserved it, and mercy is all I ask for." "Well, then," said Napoleon, "I will have mercy and pardon your son." And he did.

We, too, need mercy — not justice — and, hence, we cry out, "Have mercy upon me, O God, according to thy lovingkindness: according unto the multitude of thy tender mercies blot out my transgressions" (Psa. 51:1). In our effort to develop bigness of character, let us not forget that God "shall execute judgment without mercy, to those that hath showed no mercy" (Jas. 2:13).

VIII. THE MORE ABUNDANT LIFE IS UNAFRAID

1. *Fear is one of the greatest adversaries of the happy and successful life.* The whole creation is afflicted with fear. Everywhere you turn, fear! fear! fear! Some fear disease; others fear starvation; some fear society's condemnation; some fear earthly burdens; many fear death.

2. *Fear is overcome by faith, hope and love* (I Cor. 13:13).

(1) Our faith in God sustains us, "I had fainted unless I had believed" (Psa. 27:13).

(2) Hope serves as an anchor for the soul. "Which hope we have as an anchor of the soul, both sure and steadfast" (Heb. 6:19).

(3) Love casts out fear. "There is no fear in love; but perfect love casteth out fear" (I Jno. 4:18).

3. *Be of good courage.* You may lose a few battles without losing the war.

REVIEW EXERCISE

1. Why did the Psalmist say that he would fear no evil? ....

2. Why should we not let our hearts be troubled? ....

3. Why did Joseph call the name of his firstborn Manasseh? ....

4. What kept the Psalmist from fainting? ....

5. What does the Bible say that casts out fear? ....

6. How will God judge those who have no mercy? ....

7. Quote a passage which should make mote-hunting less attractive. ....

8. Paul in admitting his error stated that he "did it ...."

9. Quote a passage which tells of the sin of omission............................

10. Paul said, "For me to live is ...."

11. "For wherein thou judgest another, thou ...."

    Scripture:................................

12. Name four great men who made "bad" mistakes. (1)........................

(2).................................... (3) .... (4) ....

13. (T or F) For a Christian who has wronged another to be pardoned he must confess to both God and the cne wronged.

14. (T or F) Forgiveness is a matter of mercy rather than justice.

15. (T or F) Education will save us from many sorrows.

16. Thought question: What do you want out of life and how do you plan to get it?

II
The Problem of Discernment

I. INTRODUCTION

GOD has said, "But strong meat belongeth to them that are of full age, even those who by reason of use have their senses exercised to discern both good and evil" (Heb. 5:14).

1. *Discern means to see and identify by noting differences.* I must distinguish good from evil, right from wrong and truth from error.

2. *This is not a problem of choosing between the pleasant and unpleasant,* but rather between the good and the bad. What may be pleasant may be bad, and what may be unpleasant may be good. So the problem is not one of choosing that which necessarily pleases me but of choosing that which is best for me and others, the church and the gospel. That should please me, though I may sometimes wonder why it is necessary that I be tried by fire.

3. *"By reason of use" means by reason of practice or habit.* That is what the Greek word means. Long practice with the right standards enables the Christian to effect the right discernment. The Christian's mental faculties exercised at first on simple truths become a practice or habit which increases his power later to apprehend the higher and more recondite ones. Because the Hebrew Christians had failed to bring out their faculties which increase with practice, they were open to the criticism of still being spiritual infants in need of milk rather than strong meat.

For the good of my soul, I need to develop the habit of weighing matters. "An ounce of prevention is worth a pound of cure." Much trouble can be prevented through farsighted discernment.

4. *Great men have blundered because of faulty discernment.* "Great men are not always wise: neither do the aged understand judgment" (Job 32:9). They were great in spite of their mistakes; but to the extent they faltered in discernment, they decreased their greatness.

II. GOOD AND EVIL

1. *The majority are against any attempt to classify good and evil, as taught in Hebrews* 5:14. To them, nearly all moral practices are good and almost all religious teachings are right. To them, the right or wrong of an act or teaching is not in the deed or precept but rather in the mind of the participant or instructor, and thus what may be right for one may be wrong for another and vice versa. According to them, every person is a god unto himself. If this were true, no man could ever choose evil provided he thought he was choosing good, and no way which seems right could ever be wrong. In contrast, the Bible says, "There is a way which seemeth right unto a man; but the end thereof are the ways of death" (Prov. 14:12).

Some ways are good and some are bad; and the bad way has its penalty in spite of how inviting it first seems to the traveler. Switching and perverting the road signs will not make a bad road good or a good road bad, but it will bring woe upon the perpetrator. God says so: "Woe unto them that call evil good, and good evil; that put darkness for light, and light for darkness; that put bitter for sweet, and sweet for bitter" (Isa. 5:20).

2. *So the right or wrong of a thing is not just a matter of personal thinking.* Since truth and right are facts

rather than abstractions, then I must change my mind to fit them rather than change them to fit my mind. Perhaps the greatest sin of the age is man's futile attempt to change right to fit himself rather than change himself to fit right.

3. *The Bible freely speaks of the good and the evil*:

>Good man (Psa. 37:23) — evil man (Psa. 140:1).
>Good works (Matt. 5:16) — evil works (Jas. 3:16).
>Good works (I Ki. 12:7) — evil speaking (Eph. 4:31).
>Good path (Prov. 2:9) — evil ccurse (Jer. 23:10).
>Good advice (Prov. 20:18) — evil counsel (Isa. 7:5).
>Good name (Prov. 22:1) — evil name (Deut. 22:19).
>Good fruit (Matt. 7:17) — evil fruit (Matt. 7:18).
>Good heart (Lk. 8:15) — evil heart (Heb. 10:22).
>Good morals (I Cor. 15:33) — evil dealings (I Sam. 2:23).
>Good report (Phil. 4:8) — evil report (II Cor. 6:8).

III. BIBLICAL FAILURES IN DISCERNMENT

1. *The young prophet deceived by a lie* (I Ki. 13). He was one of the finest specimens of humanity. He is called "a man of God." He had courage — cried out against King Jeroboam's idolatry at Bethel, not fearing his own life. God had commanded him to neither eat nor drink nor return the same way (ver 9) and he obeyed to a point. He could not be taken in by flattery — refused an invitation to be a guest of the king. Obedience to God meant more to him than royal honors. But an old prophet turned his mind. How? He ran after him and told him an angel said, "Bring him back with thee into thine house, that he may eat bread and drink water" (ver. 18). "But he lied unto him." It cost the young prophet his life. His downfall is wrapped up in one statement: He failed in discernment. He believed a lie.

2. *The rich man who was called a fool* (Lk. 12:16-21). He was smart enough to make money, but he was not smart enough to discern material and spiritual values. He en-

joyed such a bountiful harvest his barns ran over. Then he planned to build bigger barns and fill them and say, "Soul, thou hast much goods laid up for many years; take thine ease, eat, drink, and be merry." But God called him a fool and told him that he would die that night. He was a fool because (1) he left God out of his life, and (2) he thought his soul could live on the things stored in a barn. His tragedy was one of discernment.

3. *Some tricky Pharisees who tried to trap Jesus* (Matt. 22:15-22). Because they could not comprehend two loyalties, earthly and heavenly, they thought Jesus could not. So away they went to Him with their entangling question: "Is it lawful to give tribute unto Caesar, or not?" Our Lord answered, "Render therefore unto Caesar the things which are Caesar's; and unto God the things that are God's." Analytical discrimination showed there is a place for both allegiances.

4. *Martha* (Lk. 10:38-42). She had to choose between two important things: preparing a meal or listening to Jesus. She chose the less important activity. Her sister, however, sat at Jesus' feet, and heard his word. Then Jesus kindly talked to them about which one had the finer perception and the greater power of discernment. He said, "Martha, Martha, thou art careful and troubled about many things: But one thing is needful; and Mary hath chosen that good part, which shall not be taken away from her."

5. *The "Uplift Society" that sought to stone a poor woman* (Jno. 8:3-11). These self-righteous, ever-ready condemners of others brought to Jesus a woman taken in adultery. Oh, they strutted in their piety, claiming to be sticklers for the law of Moses. They reminded Jesus that the law of Moses demanded stoning and pressed him for his verdict in the case, trying to get aught against him. Jesus answered them: "He that is without sin among you,

let him first cast a stone at her." It was then that they had business elsewhere. Brother Pray Long remembered that he had promised to meet his wife in town. It just dawned on Brother Firm Ritual that he was running late for an appointment at the bank. Brother Helping Hand suddenly realized that he would have to hurry home and get his notes on his speech, "Helping Those Who Fall," which he was soon to give at a meeting of the Big Brother and Sister Society. No doubt each had an excuse. Actually, each left because of his conscience.

They made lots of mistakes, and basically because they erred in their discernment:

Mistake Number One — they did not bring the man.

Mistake Number Two — they made a spectacle by setting her in the midst of the crowd.

Mistake Number Three — they did not care whom they hurt just so they carried their point.

Mistake Number Four — they beheld the sin in another's life, but failed to see the more numerous sins in their own lives.

Mistake Number Five — they pointed to another's sin in an effort to feel bigger and cleaner, to whitewash themselves.

Jesus discerned the matter properly by showing less concern for the woman's past than for her future. He said to her, "Neither do I condemn thee: go, and sin no more."

6. *The Pharisees in Matthew* 23. Bear in mind they were religious people. Jesus indicted them several times for their erroneous discernment, three of which we shall mention:

Indictment Number One — "Ye pay tithe of mint and anise and cummin, and have omitted the weightier matters of the law, judgment, mercy, and faith: these ought ye to have done, and not to leave the other undone" (ver. 23).

Indictment Number Two — "Ye blind guides, which strain at a gnat, and swallow a camel" (ver. 24).

Indictment Number Three — "Ye make clean the outside of the cup and of the platter, but within they are full of extortion and excess" (ver. 25).

IV. GUIDEPOSTS TO WISE DISCERNMENT

1. *Faith.* One of the greatest examples of perception is Moses and the causative force in his life was faith. "By faith Moses, when he was come to years, refused to be called the son of Pharaoh's daughter; choosing rather to suffer affliction with the people of God, than to enjoy the pleasures of sin for a season" (Heb. 11:24,25). Faith led him to make the right decision.

2. *Hope* was another power which influenced Moses in his choice. "For he had respect unto the recompense of the reward" (Heb. 11:26).

3. *Love.* Jesus said, "If a man love me, he will keep my words" (Jno. 14:23). A greater love for human glory than for God was the deciding factor which caused some rulers to reject Christ (Jno. 12:42, 43). The Bible speaks of "lovers of pleasures more than lovers of God" (II Tim. 3:4) — is this speaking of any one of us? Paul said that those who love not the truth will not find the truth, but rather will be possessed with a delusion which will cause them to believe a lie and be damned (II Thess. 2:10-12).

4. *Courage.* "Fear not them which kill the body, but are not able to kill the soul" (Matt. 10:28) — this will surely help me in making the right decision. The Christian's big problem is to do right and buy the truth, let

the world do what it will. "Buy the truth, and sell it not" (Prov. 23:23). Fear has often gotten in the way of wise judgments: fear of financial loss, fear of job loss, fear of promotion loss, fear of prestige loss, fear of public favor loss, fear of persecution, fear of ridicule, fear of life. Saul explained his great disobedience with one word, fear: "I feared the people, and obeyed their voice" (I Sam. 15:24).

5. *Examples of Jesus.* It was prophesied of Christ: "He may know to refuse the evil, and choose the good" (Isa. 7:15). He is the only man who ever perfectly discerned every problem and every issue of life. He "was in all points tempted like as we are, yet without sin" (Heb. 4:15). The devil and all his friends, the combined forces of the opposition, hounded him, tested him, tried him, tempted him, persecuted him and crucified him, but he was able to take everything they could hand out, answering every question and handling every matter and every circumstance with perfection. To the extent we follow the principles Christ laid down, we shall be wise discerners.

6. *Sincerity* rather than deceit. Love unfeigned, love free of hypocrisy, enables one to make a better decision than if he is moved by deceit. It will free him of retaliation, vengeance and many other woes which cloud the judgment.

7. *Caution.* "Watch ye" (I Cor. 16:13). "A prudent man foreseeth the evil, and hideth himself: but the simple pass on, and are punished" (Prov. 22:3). What looks good may not be good. Solomon said that which appears to be sweet bread may be gravel.

8. *Investigation.* Never reach a decision of consequence without fully investigating. I should be sure I have the facts before condemning others or before plotting a course for myself. I must deal with knowledge instead of pre-

sumption, gossip or rumors. Gullible men have bought stocks on rumors and lost. Men and women have repeated tales without investigating which falsely damaged reputations. People have accepted doctrines without searching the Scriptures. But this rashness is not the behavior of the prudent person. "Every prudent man dealeth with knowledge" (Prov. 13:16). The Bereans acted with prudence. They searched the Scriptures daily to see if what they were hearing was true (Acts 17:11).

9. *Principles* rather than abuses of principles. Right here is where so many people err. They start out to fight the abuse of a principle and end up fighting the principle. They throw out the baby with the wash. Every good thing has its dangers, even the pulpit. It is the Christian's duty to discern good and evil, throw out the evil and retain the good. Much trouble has arisen in the church because of poor discernment. One of the daily and most urgent problems of the Christian is discernment.

REVIEW EXERCISE

1. What is the meaning of "discern"?..

2. Can a way that seems right be wrong?............ Scripture:..................

3. What is God's pronouncement upon these who call evil good, and good evil?.. Scripture:...........................

4. What was the thing that doomed the young prophet?.......................

5. How did Martha fail in her discernment?..

6. What two things enabled Moses to discern wisely?..........................

7. What does courage have to do with discernment?..........................

8. "Great men are not always ....: neither do the aged ...." Scripture: ....

9. State two reasons why the rich man in Luke 12 was a fool:
   (1) .... (2) ....

10. Give the discernment our Lord made of loyalties in response to the question: "Is it lawful to give tribute unto Caesar, or not?"
    ....

11. Give at least four mistakes of those who sought to stone the adulterous woman.
    (1) ....
    (2) ....
    (3) ....
    (4) ....

12. Jesus said the Pharisees "omitted the weightier matters of the law, ..., ..., and ....

13. (T or F) The Bereans were not investigators of the truth.

14. (T or F) Jesus called some religious leaders "blind guides."

15. (T or F) Inasmuch as some things are good and some are evil, then the right or wrong of a thing is not just a matter of personal thinking.

16. Thought question: What has discernment done for you?

III
The Problem of Immaturity

I. INTRODUCTION

WE shall ever have the problem of putting away childish things. Paul said, "When I was a child, I spake as a child, I understood as a child, I thought as a child: but when I became a man, I put away childish things" (I Cor. 13:11). It is a God-given duty to grow up. Our Christian calling demands that we be big men and women. Christianity is too big and great to be defiled by the petty littleness of bantam-sized personalities housed in full-grown bodies. It is proper for children to act like children, but it is improper for people who are grown in body to remain children in disposition — that is not good. Adults should behave as adults. This does not come without effort; so we should daily work at the problem of personality improvement lest we revert to the traits of our young and undeveloped lives.

II. CHILDISH TRAITS WE SHOULD RETAIN

There are some characteristics of childhood we should cherish and hold fast all our lives, but there are others we should outgrow as quickly as possible. However, unless we are watchful and desirous of the more beautiful life, we shall lose the good and keep the bad traits of immaturity. Here are some of the sweet and tender traits of little children that should be ours forever.

1. *Simple faith and trust.* Little children have a natural tendency to believe what people tell them and to trust them to the fullest. Several years ago a father and his

little son had the hair-raising experience of being in a wagon hitched to a runaway team. It was a horrifying experience for the father who tried to manage the team lest his son be killed. But the child later commented, "I wasn't afraid, because my daddy was with me." Trust in the father's love and power had driven out all fear. This kind of trust in our heavenly Father will also protect us from fright. "I will trust and not be afraid" (Isa. 12:2). One of the greatest pieces of advice in all the world for life's everyday bumps is found in Proverbs 3:5,6: "Trust in the Lord with all thine heart; and lean not unto thine own understanding. In all thy ways acknowledge him, and he shall direct thy paths."

2. *Sympathy.* Children are very compassionate and tender-hearted. They are easily touched by the sufferings of any living creature, and we have seen it manifested so often toward a crippled bird, a mangy dog or a half-starved kitten.

We, too, should be moved by the infirmities and misfortunes of our fellow beings. One of the most expressive Scriptures on right attitudes is Romans 12:15: "Rejoice with them that do rejoice, and weep with them that weep." That is the Christian spirit. It will save us from envy, jealousy and hardness which are the roots of many other sins. Life is so much sweeter for everyone concerned when we are "kind one to another, tender-hearted" (Eph. 4:32).

3. *Forgiveness.* The little ones can fuss and fight and go back to playing together in thirty minutes. They are so genuine and sincere in their manifestation of forgiveness — no grudges. They do not play the hypocrite of pretending to have forgiven while all the time they are secretly seeking an opportunity to retaliate. When God forgives he forgets (Heb. 10:17); and no less is expected of us, for that is one of the marks of true forgiveness. We

must forgive even as Christ forgave us. "Forbearing one another, and forgiving one another, if any man have a quarrel against any: even as Christ forgave you, so also do ye" (Col. 3:13). And we have no right to ask God to extend us a forgiveness we are unwilling to practice toward others. This is fair: "And forgive us our debts, as we forgive our debtors" (Matt. 6:12).

III. SOME CHILDISH THINGS WE SHOULD PUT AWAY

Now that we have become men and women and for a greater reason — we have been born again — we should consider it a daily challenge to rid ourselves and keep ourselves free of all undesirable traits of immaturity. Let us become too big for the following:

1. *Tattling.* A child is disposed to tattle. He gossips because he thinks it will stand him in good with the person to whom he is talking, not being mature enough to comprehend what it may do to somebody else. We can overlook it in a child, but we cannot disregard it in an adult who failed to grow up.

It has ever been God's will that man refrain from talebearing: "Thou shalt not go up and down as a talebearer among thy people" (Lev. 19:16). Tattling is a stock in trade of idlers and busybodies and the three are mentioned together in the same Scripture: "And withal they learn to be idle, wandering about from house to house; and not only idle, but tattlers also and busybodies, speaking things which they ought not" (I Tim. 5:13). Thus it is evident from the passage that two excellent ways to overcome tattling is (1) go to work and (2) stay out of the other fellow's business.

2. *Vainglory.* It is characteristic of children to want attention. Children need to be loved, but too much attention warps their personalities. A few years ago while vis-

iting in a home, I observed a little boy who demonstrated that he thought he was not getting enough attention; but I could not do much about it because his parents were controlling the conversation. Finally he walked over to a table and jerked a scarf upon which there was a lamp. It broke the lamp, but he got attention. Sometimes children will act mean in class just to be noticed; and if the bystanders laugh, it encourages them to be meaner. Much of the reckless driving on the part of some teenagers is just to focus attention on themselves.

Some adults are too much obsessed with the desire for special attention. They think the whole world revolves around them and you had better be one of the spokes, or anathematized you will be. God has said, "Let us not be desirous of vainglory, provoking one another, envying one another" (Gal. 5:26). He has further given us the solution to the problem — humility: "Humble yourselves therefore under the mighty hand of God" (I Pet. 5:6).

3. *Envy and jealousy*. We saw a little boy step on a playmate's new shoes — his shoes were not new. We witnessed a little girl's throwing water on another one who had a new dress — the obvious reason was she did not have a new dress.

Adults may be envious of another's success, business, clothes and looks. Envy among adults is an internal, rotten condition. "But envy is the rottenness of the bones" (Prov. 14:30). Envy crucified Christ (Matt. 27:18) and continues to crucify his disciples.

4. *All play and no work*. Children do not like to work. They like to play. To them life is just one big game and the world is a huge playhouse. We do our children an injustice if we fail to teach them to work.

Many adults have not grown out of this irresponsible

state of childhood. They just want to play in life, accept no responsibilities, let the other fellow bear all the burdens. They want to receive much from the world without giving an equal amount in return. But God's law of life is a law of labor. All other things being equal, a man should not expect to eat if he has not worked, and God said so: "If any would not work, neither should he eat" (II Thess. 3:10).

The little ones in their childish pastime play church. Many of their parents do the same — just play church rather than work at the calling. A lot of growing up is needed in church work. "Work out your own salvation with fear and trembling" (Phil. 2:12).

5. *Instability.* Children are very changeable and inconstant. You can put one to work, but it is hard to keep him at it. He finds it difficult to finish a job.

We realize that it is not easy to stick with a difficult responsibility, but that is one of the tests of a mature person.

Successful living demands steadfastness. The wishy-washy, fickle person can never meet the demands of God's program for life in either the physical or spiritual realms. Triumphant living is found in this steady principle: "Be ye steadfast, unmovable, always abounding in the work of the Lord" (I Cor. 15:58).

6. *Wrangling.* Children have the disposition to argue, fuss and quarrel; furthermore, they seem to enjoy it. They will argue about anything: whose daddy is the stronger or who makes more money or whose mother is better looking. And they will do more than debate the issue — we have seen them stand and throw rocks at each other.

There are also many fussy adults who have not matured

out of this childish state; and they, too, seem to enjoy it. There was a young husband who said to his wife, "Let's not fuss tonight. I feel awfully bad. Why don't you wait until I get to feeling better so I can enjoy it?"

One of the hateful and abominable things in the sight of God is the sowing of "discord among brethren" (Prov. 6:19). One of our everyday problems is to "seek peace, and ensue it" (I Pet. 3:11). With some people peace is impossible; but "if it be possible, as much as lieth in you, live peaceably with all men" (Rom. 12:18). "Let us therefore follow after the things which make for peace, and things wherewith one may edify another" (Rom. 14:19).

7. *Discourtesy.* One of the characteristics of the younger years is rudeness — in fact, children can be very cruel. They sometimes are so ill-mannered as to stand off and sing, "Johnny is a sissy" or "Mary's hair looks like a horse's tail." What harshness! And even though Johnny and Mary are just children, the wound hurts.

Some adults live in a similar state of immaturity: mature in body, but immature in emotions. They get a perverted satisfaction out of criticizing and chiding others. Their joy comes from inflicting wounds instead of binding them up. It is their disposition to make people weep rather than "weep with them that weep" (Rom. 12:15). No matter what they claim, they are the opposite image of the Christian. Love will not permit an unkind course of action. "Love suffereth long, and is kind" (I Cor. 13:4). But it is hard for some people to love others because they are so much in love with themselves.

Nothing costs so little and is so priceless as courtesy.

8. *Sullenness.* Children are excellent pouters. They enjoy feeling they have been mistreated. If you forget

THE PROBLEM OF IMMATURITY

one's birthday or accidentally step on him under your feet, he enjoys feeling he has been neglected or abused.

Some adults are no different. They get more joy out of an oversight than an invitation to some function. When they are sick and do not notify their friends and consequently have only a few visitors, they have a good time telling everybody they have been mistreated. The inconsistency of their wanting attention during their illness when they themselves have never visited the sick very much does not seem to bother them — they want better treatment than they are willing to give.

The great sin of the older brother in the Parable of the Prodigal Son was pouting (Lk. 15:25-32).

IV. CONCLUSION

As a summary let us keep in mind the command, "Quit you like men" (I Cor. 16:13). When I was a boy and did something wrong my mother or father would say, "Quit that." I thought *quit* meant *stop*, but it really means *behave*. We are commanded to behave as men, and there is a big difference in the behavior of a man and a child. It is a daily duty to behave as adults. Let us act our age.

REVIEW EXERCISE

1. What did Paul do when he became a man? _____

2. "If any man have a quarrel," what should he do? _____

3. What is one of the hateful and abominable things in the sight of God? _____

4. What should be our attitude toward those that weep? _____

5. What was the great sin of the older brother in the Parable of the Prodigal Son? _____

THE CHRISTIAN'S EVERYDAY PROBLEMS

6. Quote a passage which teaches we should "not be desirous of vainglory." ....

7. What is the danger of idlers wandering from house to house? ....

8. Give three childish traits we should retain. ....

9. Trust expels .... (Isa. 12:2).

10. When God forgives he .... (Heb. 10:17).

11. Quote a passage which teaches that we should be stable and constant. ....

12. We are taught to "follow after the things which make for........... ...."

13. (T or F) Paul said that we should stop like men.

14. (T or F) God will forgive us even though we are unwilling to forgive others.

15. (T or F) It is not the duty of church members to edify one another.

16. Thought question: What practical suggestions can you give that will aid us in becoming more mature?

IV
The Problem of Worry

I. INTRODUCTION

ANOTHER one of the everyday problems of the Christian is worry, fretfulness, anxiety and care. I must work daily to overcome it and keep it from overcoming me. Life can be harassed with worry or beautified with contentment, depending upon how I make it; for both are inside jobs. Of course, there are outside influences that may encourage and prod us to be anxious and gloomy, but we do not have to open our hearts to the pressures which are sure to torment us.

To some extent, we are creatures of habit. Years ago a mother and a daughter got into the habit of writing to each other the gloomiest, most depressing and most apprehensive letters imaginable. It seemed that they were in a contest to see which one could write the most troubled letter. Seldom ever was there any sunshine in their correspondence. Worry had become a way of life, so much so that it seemed they were enjoying their low spirits. While it is true that the mother had stamped the heart of her daughter with anxiety, it is still true that it was an inside job on the part of the daughter; for worry can only work within us. In both cases, great amounts of time and energy were being drained uselessly.

The habit of fretting had so taken hold of one man that he often worried because he had forgotten what he was supposed to worry about.

God does not want his children to be anxious. He has spoken:

"Be careful [anxious] for nothing; but in everything by prayer and supplication with thanksgiving let your requests be made known unto God" (Phil. 4:6).

"Casting all your care upon him; for he careth for you" (I Pet. 5:7).

II. OVERCOMING WORRY

Inasmuch as worry is a thought process, then it is reasonable to assume that we can control it by changing our thinking, by thinking upon the things which are antipodal to the thoughts which produce anxiety. Now let us think upon the worry preventives and antidotes. They serve both purposes — preventives for those who are not worrying and antidotes for those who are.

1. *Much faith repels worry, while little faith invites it.* Sometimes we believe our doubts and doubt our beliefs. This was true of Peter who began to walk on the water. When he saw that the wind was boisterous he became afraid and began to sink. Jesus, taking him by the hand, said to him, "O thou of little faith, wherefore didst thou doubt?" (Matt. 14:31). Our sea of life also has its boisterous winds. There are so many storm clouds to try our faith. If our faith breaks, our anxiety forms.

We need to believe that the God who feeds the birds and clothes the grass of the field will care for us (Matt. 6:25-31). This is why Jesus told us not to be anxious for our lives, what we shall eat and what we shall wear.

OVERHEARD IN AN ORCHARD

Said the robin to the sparrow,
"I should really like to know
Why these anxious human beings
Rush about, and worry so?"

> Said the sparrow to the robin,
> "Friend, I think that it must be
> They have no heavenly Father
> Such as cares for you and me."
>
> — Elizabeth Cheyney

2. *Trust in the Lord keeps spirits from dropping low.* It gives us the blessing of sustenance and security, though adversaries threaten us. "Blessed is the man that trusteth in the Lord, and whose hope the Lord is. For he shall be as a tree planted by the waters, and that spreadeth out her roots by the river, and shall not see when heat cometh, but her leaf shall be green; and shall not be careful in the year of drought, neither shall cease from yielding fruit" (Jer. 17:7,8). What striking and comprehensible language — a tree with green leaves and fruit, which sees no heat and knows no drought, because its roots are fed by the river of waters; and this was said to picture to us the nourishing power of trust in God.

Occasionally we are brought face to face with besetting experiences we cannot understand, but we can trust Him who has never betrayed a trust. "Trust in the Lord with all thine heart; and lean not unto thine own understanding" (Prov. 3:5).

An example is in order: All through life we trust our safety to bridges built by man. The supporting piers are deep down beneath the water. We do not doubt their strength. We do not worry when they tremble or swerve in the storm — we trust the builder. Significantly but vitally more important, life's highway has its bridges resting deep down in the wisdom of God, hidden in the depths of time and eternity. No bridge of God ever collapsed. It is easy to trust the bridge, if I really trust the Builder.

An elderly man, after many years of trustfulness, went

through his Bible and wrote "proved" by every promise or bridge God has given to support man in time of trial and distress. Experiences had proved that God is true.

One of the sweetest tributes to the vitalizing power of trust in God is the beautiful twenty-third Psalm: "The Lord is my shepherd; I shall not want . . . I will fear no evil . . . my cup runneth over . . ."

I know not the future, but I know the God who is in it — then do not worry.

3. *An acceptance of self helps to prevent fretfulness.* Jesus asked, "Which of you by taking thought can add one cubit to his stature?" (Matt. 6:27). Worrying about your height will not change it. We are on the road to contentment if we accept ourselves as we are, even though we have severe handicaps.

A lady once said that the happiest day of her life was the day she accepted the fact that she could never be a beauty queen. She was a beautiful woman, but there were imperfections which kept her from winning beauty titles. As long as she strove for that which was beyond her reach, her days were haunted with bafflement and frustration. An acceptance of self brought peace.

Realistic living demands that we accept the fact that different people have different talents and various degrees of ability. Our world is still one in which some are given five talents; some, two; and others, one (Matt. 25:14-30). Even though we are one-talent persons, we must accept it. Complaining about what we do not have will not give us more. Aspiration unrealistically in excess of ability will make life gloomy and hopeless. Ambition is needed, but so is realism. It is good to reach for a star, provided one keeps his feet on the ground.

An acceptance of self enables us to be ourselves, and

this is a prerequisite to peace of mind. Many people worry themselves sick trying to be something they are not.

4. *Faith in self helps to prevent worry.* It is scriptural to say, "I can," provided one is linked to the Lord. Paul said, "I can do all things through Christ which strengtheneth me" (Phil. 4:13). Can is the victor's word; can't is the word of the vanquished.

Truly it takes much strength to live up to our responsibilities in life. But strength, physical, moral and spiritual, is a growing quality. The more we use it, the more we have; so strength develops proportionately to our needs. "As thy days, so shall thy strength be" (Deut. 33:25).

We have watched the steam locomotive hitched to a long string of cars pull away on the tracks. It did not have enough steam to make the trip. The engineer knew this, but he began the journey on faith. He knew there was fuel and more steam could be produced. God does not give us enough power at the first of life's journey to take us through; but he does give us fuel from which more power can be generated as we travel. Then do not worry.

I should not worry about performing my duties. All that is expected of me is to do the best I can; when I have done that, I have succeeded.

> The world is wide
> In time and tide,
> And God is guide,
>   Then — do not hurry.
> That man is blest
> Who does his best
> And leaves the rest,
>   Then — do not worry.
>
> — Charles F. Deems

5. *Planning and making the day-before preparation is a*

safeguard against many worrisome problems. Jesus said, "For which of you, intending to build a tower, sitteth down first, and counteth the cost, whether he have sufficient to finish it? Lest haply, after he hath laid the foundation, and is not able to finish it, all that behold it begin to mock him, saying, This man began to build, and was not able to finish" (Lk. 14:28-30). Then he had something to worry about, but it could have been prevented.

General Foch said, "Battles are won the day before." We need the day-before preparation.

Plan the work and work the plan — then there won't be so much to worry about.

6. *Casting our burdens upon the Lord relieves us of the heavy weights of anxiety.* "Cast thy burden upon the Lord, and he shall sustain thee: he shall never suffer the righteous to be moved" (Psa. 55:22). Life has its complications. There are many problems which seem to defy solution, and in time we shall be pressed beneath them unless we learn to shift them to the Lord. This is the only way we can hold up.

The camel which bears heavy burdens during the long, toilsome day will kneel at night before his master for the burdens to be removed. To bear the load day and night would soon break down a beast of burden.

We also need to kneel at night before our Master that our burdens may be lifted. "Ye have not, because ye ask not" (Jas. 4:2). You have not your burdens lifted, because you ask not that they be lifted.

7. *My counting my blessings instead of my supposed misfortunes enables me to see how well off I really am instead of how bad off I may think I am.* It is then that I can say, "Blessed be the Lord, who daily loadeth us with

benefits, even the God of our salvation" (Psa. 68:19). So we are not nearly loaded with cares like we are with benefits. By being thankful for what I have, I am not so apt to fret about what I do not have. There is a great blessing in counting my blessings.

> Are you ever burdened with a load of care?
> Does the cross seem heavy you are called to bear?
> Count your many blessings, name them one by one.

Count your benefits instead of your reverses, and it will surprise you how your efficiency and personality improve.

"Be ye thankful" (Col. 3:15). Thankfulness makes the man and shows the man.

8. *Living life a day at a time will spare me many misgivings.* Jesus said, "Be not therefore anxious for the morrow: for the morrow will be anxious for itself. Sufficient unto the day is the evil thereof" (Matt. 6:34, A.S.V.). Jesus was not rebuking preparation for the future, but rather anxiety. After all, the best preparation any person can make for tomorrow is to do what needs to be done today.

The Master aimed the passage at the common mistake of trying to live life in the lump. Trying to solve today the problems of a lifetime is enough to worry and frighten any person to the breaking point. Today has enough of its own burdens without our piling on ourselves the ones years ahead. Some people cannot efficiently do their duties today for worrying about tomorrow — this is what Jesus reprimanded.

9. *My cultivating myself to see good instead of evil in the world is a shield against the darts of worry.* "An ungodly man diggeth up evil" (Prov. 16:27). So if I complain about the evil in others, I may actually be complaining about the evil that exists in me. I am not suggesting

that we should not be realistic, but I am suggesting that what we often see is only a reflection of ourselves. We may see good because we are good; evil, because we are possessed with evil; defeat, because we are defeated; fear, because we are afraid; and clouds, because we have a haze over our eyes. We have taken a long step toward overcoming anxiety when we can see cloudy days as bright days with nothing more than a mask on.

There are so many good things in this world — all I need is to train my eyes to see them. As I see more good, I see less cause to worry.

>   My God, I thank thee who hast made
>   The earth so bright,
>   So full of splendor and of joy,
>   Beauty and light;
>   So many glorious things are here,
>   Noble and right.
>   — Adelaide A. Procter

I should not put on a long face and expect the worst, but contrariwise I should wear a smile and anticipate the best. If I smile at the world, the world will smile back at me; so one of my daily problems is to smile and keep the right outlook on life.

>   Keep your face with sunshine lit,
>   Laugh a little bit!
>   Gloomy shadows oft will flit,
>   If you have the wit and grit
>   Just to laugh a little bit!
>   — J. B. Cook

REVIEW EXERCISE

1. What did Jesus say to Peter when he began to sink? ....

2. What lesson was the Lord teaching when he mentioned God's feeding the birds? ....

THE PROBLEM OF WORRY

3. To what did Jeremiah compare the man who trusts the Lord?
....

4. What does the twenty-third Psalm teach us about trust in God?
....

5. Why did Paul have faith in himself? ....

6. What was Jesus rebuking when he taught man to live a day at a time? ....

7. What may be the real evil when one complains about evil in others? ....

8. Give the reason Peter gave for our casting our care upon God.
....

Scripture:......................................

9. "Blessed be the Lord, who .... loadeth us with ...." Scripture:...

10. Paul stated that we should be careful or anxious for............................
Scripture:..

11. Give the question Jesus asked in teaching man to accept self.
....

12. "Cast thy .... upon the Lord, and he shall............................ thee: he shall never suffer the .... to be ...." (Psa. 55:22).

13. (T or F) Worry is an inside job.

14. (T or F) Jesus taught that man should plan before he begins to build.

15. (T or F) Our strength can never grow in proportion to our needs.

16. Thought question: Have you ever solved a problem by worrying?

V
The Problem of Enemies

I. INTRODUCTION

IT is an honor to have friends; but it is not necessarily a dishonor to have enemies. In some cases it is as complimentary to have enemies as friends. Just as you can tell a man by his friends, you can sometimes tell a man by his enemies. Birds of a feather fly together; the same kind of fish swim in schools; and there is a special affinity among various kinds of people.

It is no compliment to say that a Christian lived so many years and never had an enemy. This could not be said of Christ or Paul. The Bible says, "Yea, and all that will live godly in Christ Jesus shall suffer persecution" (II Tim. 3:12). Human nature has not changed — the persecution will come, though the form may be different. But fret not. For "woe unto you, when all men shall speak well of you!" (Lk. 6:26).

II. ENEMIES WITHOUT CAUSE

Yes, enemies without cause! The Psalmist said, "Let not them that are mine enemies wrongfully rejoice over me: neither let them wink the eye that hate me without cause" (Psa. 35:19).

The trouble is in their hearts. Job said, "But ye should say, Why persecute we him, seeing the root of the matter is found in me?" (Job 19:28).

Thus it is evident that we may have enemies when it is not our fault. For instance:

1. *One reason is the unfairness of unreasonable people.* Paul said, "Finally, brethren, pray for us . . . that we may be delivered from unreasonable and wicked men: for all men have not faith" (II Thess. 3:2).

Innocent people have been unjustly blamed because of the false notion that enmity is about half the fault of one and half the fault of the other. Nothing is further from the truth. Inasmuch as friendship is a reasonable relationship, then it is almost impossible to have a lasting friendship with an unreasonable person.

People devoid of reason are filled with enmity, hate, resentment, bitterness and vengeance. What they condemn in others, true or false, often is only their subconscious way of condemning the same evil in their own hearts. In their perverted condition they have a strong compulsion to hate and fight someone. They need a whipping-boy; and if you have been elected, you have been whipped without just cause.

2. *You may have an enemy for the simple reason he or she experienced a slip of the tongue and talked about you.* The Bible says, "A lying tongue hateth those that are afflicted by it" (Prov. 26:28). After talking about you, the loose-tongued person began to build up opposition to you in his mind in an effort to justify the wrong done you. Instead of changing his tongue, he changed his image of the person his tongue hurt in an effort to make the person correspond to what he said about him. The barrier was down; and as time went on, there was more talking and consequently more enmity. It became an endless circle of talk and hate and hate and talk. Its roots are found in criticism and gossip.

3. *You may have an enemy because he mistreated you or did you harm.* After first doing you evil, he began to

fight you in an effort to justify the wrong committed; he rationalized that he really did no wrong, that you are an evil person who deserves to be opposed and fought. So actually he wrestled with his own sins — of course, in the wrong way — by fighting you.

There are so many first wrongs which can start the guilty person on the road to hating the innocent. (1) It may result from a debt that is not paid. The debtor becomes the enemy of his creditor, but the creditor has done him no harm. (2) It can be caused by misrepresentation regarding a transaction whereby one is cheated. The cheater hates the cheated because he knows that the one he has wronged knows him for what he is. (3) It can occur because of exorbitant prices charged for services rendered. The person who overcharges you for repairs on plumbing, wiring and television is much more apt to hate you than the person who charges you a fair amount. Man has a tendency to like the people he treats fairly and to despise the people he treats unfairly. "It is more blessed to give than to receive" (Acts 20:35) is good in many fields. (4) It may happen because of job interference: interfering with another's promotion or even trying to get him dismissed. Then what was first a dislike of the person becomes a bitter hate and avowed enmity.

One brother in the church took advantage of another brother for whom he worked by abusing the trust placed in him. A thing like that will not remain the same. The guilty party will either confess his fault and try to make it right or begin to dislike and then hate the person he wronged. In this case, the guilty person did the latter.

One woman tried to get a man dismissed from his employment. She could apologize or fight him more. She chose the latter.

All of this could be avoided if the perpetrators of the wrongs against others had enough Christianity or even character to go to the ones they have hurt and apologize (Jas. 5:16).

4. *Enmity may result from reproof.* If it does, the enemy must be classified as a scorner instead of a wise person. Solomon said, "Reprove not a scorner, lest he hate thee; rebuke a wise man, and he will love thee" (Prov. 9:8). And Paul asked, "Am I therefore become your enemy because I tell you the truth?" (Gal. 4:16).

Every gospel preacher has had enemies because he stepped on toes; but he had no choice, for the truth had to be preached. Having friendship on the condition of compromising the truth or the right is too great a price to pay.

5. *A refusal to flatter will make enemies of some people.* It did of the king of Israel who said of Micaiah, "I hate him; for he doth not prophesy good concerning me" (I Ki. 22:8). This is especially true of the immature. They have to be flattered and bolstered all the time. It indicates self-love and vanity. No one dares to say anything to them that is uncomplimentary, no matter how truthful, lest they "turn again and rend you" (Matt. 7:6).

6. *Knowing something bad on another may cause that one to become your enemy.* A woman backed her car into another car across the street from her house. She got out of her car and looked, saw the damage done, and drove off and stayed gone about an hour and returned as if nothing had happened. But a little girl who witnessed all of it told the owner of the parked car what had occurred. The owner of the parked car went to the woman's house and told her what she had done and asked her to repair the damages. She denied doing it. He was nice about it and did not press the matter further; he never mentioned it

to her again; neither did he report it to the police. But from then on the woman hated the man and never spoke to him again. Why? Because he knew something ugly about her.

In view of this truth, I have made it a point to try to keep from learning ugly things about people. If they should learn that I know bad things about them, it would tend to make enemies. Furthermore, "An ungodly man diggeth up evil" (Prov. 16:27), and I do not wish to be put in that class.

7. *Being successful or popular may make enemies for you.* It will cause you to become the object of some people's envy. This, of course, indicates a rotten internal condition on their part for which you are not responsible. "Envy is the rottenness of the bones" (Prov. 14:30). This was Cain's trouble — internal rottenness — and it proved he "was of that wicked one" (I Jno. 3:12). Envy knows no rest.

You cannot succeed without paying the price of having some people hate you, and for no reason except you arose above them.

A farmer had many friends in his community, and seldom ever was aught said against him . . . until he became rich from oil; and in one year his supposed friends had become his enemies and were talking about him. Why? He was wealthy and they were not.

Love would have prevented this. "Love envieth not" (I Cor. 13:4).

III. ENEMIES WE HAVE MADE

While we may be innocent in having enemies we did not make, as seen in the foregoing section, we may also be guilty of having enemies we did make.

In either case, our greatest and most spiteful enemies

are those who consider us a personal threat in some manner to them: their dignity, job advancement, popularity, social standing or financial welfare. The feeling prevails: "You are interfering with my plans; you are hurting me; and I don't like you." This is why Herod sought the life of Jesus, the new-born King (Matt. 2:1-18).

One business man's conception of a good man is one who trades with him; and his conception of a bad man is one who trades with his competitor. In one case there is financial enhancement, and in the other he senses a threat to his financial welfare.

Any kind of threat to another's welfare tends to make enemies. No doubt this was the reason Diotrephes refused to receive John — he considered John a threat to his preeminence (III Jno. 9).

IV. WHAT TO DO ABOUT ENEMIES

1. *Do good unto them.* Jesus said, "Love your enemies, bless them that curse you, do good to them that hate you" (Matt. 5:44). "Therefore if thine enemy hunger, feed him; if he thirst, give him drink: for in so doing thou shalt heap coals of fire on his head" (Rom. 12:20). Never retaliate (Rom. 12:19).

David's goodness toward Saul who had done him great wrong temporarily softened the heart of Saul, and he said to David, "Thou art more righteous than I: for thou hast rewarded me good, whereas I have rewarded thee evil" (I Sam. 24:17). Though this attitude of Saul did not last, it was not the fault of David — he did right toward his enemy.

2. *Pray for them.* "Pray for them which despitefully use you, and persecute you; that ye may be the children of your Father which is in heaven" (Matt. 5:44,45). Jesus practiced what he preached. He prayed for the ones who

crucified him, "Father, forgive them; for they know not what they do" (Lk. 23:34). Stephen prayed in the same manner, "Lord, lay not this sin to their charge" (Acts 7:60). It takes much more courage to pray for your enemies than it does to knife them in the back or even to fight them openly.

Two business men were bitter enemies because they were competitors. The enmity was destroying both of them and their businesses. One of them, speaking of the other, said to the preacher, "You see Old So and So. He is the lowest down, conniving, thieving skunk in this town." The preacher said, "You don't like him . . . " And he blurted out, "Like him? I hate him." The preacher continued, "Sam, if you don't overcome this, it is going to wreck your health and ruin your business. The thing for you to do is to pray for him each night. Ask God to bless him and his business as well as you and yours." After much reasoning, the upset business man agreed that he would try. That night he prayed, "Dear God, I promised the preacher that I would try to pray for Old Skin Flint. You know I don't mean it, but I promised I would. So bless him as well as me, if you see best." The next night it was easier; and the next, still easier. In time they became the best of friends, and each one's business prospered. Each spent his time and energy building his business instead of fighting the other.

3. *Refrain from getting on the level of an enemy.* Jesus is a classic example of this. "Who, when he was reviled, reviled not again; when he suffered, he threatened not; but committed himself to him that judgeth righteously" (I Pet. 2:23). You cannot lift up others by pulling yourself down.

4. *Rejoice not at the failings of an enemy.* "Rejoice not when thine enemy falleth, and let not thine heart be

glad when he stumbleth" (Prov. 24:17). This is another one of the principles which distinguishes the godly from the ungodly. Let each measure himself by it to see what kind of person he is.

5. *Remember that it is through God's commandments you can be made wiser than your enemies.* The Psalmist said, "Thou through thy commandments hast made me wiser than mine enemies: for they are ever with me" (Psa. 119:98). By following God's instructions, we can outwit our enemies, though the persecution may try every nerve and impulse within us.

6. *We can pray for deliverance from our enemies.* This was the constant prayer of the Psalmist: "Deliver me from mine enemies, O my God: defend me from them that rise up against me" (Psa. 59:1). "Faith without works is dead" (Jas. 2:20); so let us work as well as pray. Works without prayer are also dead; so let us not forget to pray for rescue.

7. *Let us always remember that God is stronger than our enemies and can care for us despite them.* It will give us fortitude and soothe our nerves to meditate on the words of the immortal twenty-third Psalm: "Thou preparest a table before me in the presence of mine enemies."

V. CONCLUSION

I cannot always help having enemies, but I can help my attitude toward them.

REVIEW EXERCISE

1. What is the attitude of a lying tongue toward those afflicted by it? .... Scripture:................

2. What suffering did Paul say would come to those who live godly

in Christ Jesus? ....

Scripture: ....

3. If one who has wronged another is not big enough and penitent enough to confess it, what is he or she likely to do? ....

....

4. What question did Paul ask relative to the possibility of becoming the enemy of some church members? ....

....

5. Why did the king hate Micaiah? ....

6. What was Cain's internal trouble? ....

7. Why are some people our most spiteful enemies? ....

....

8. Quote the passage which speaks of enemies without a cause:

....

....

9. It is the .... man who digs up evil.

10. "Envy is the .... of the bones." Scripture:

....

11. Doing good to enemies will heap on them .... of ....

12. Through God's commandments we are made... than our enemies.

13. (T or F) It is a bad sign when all men speak well of you.

14. (T or F) The Bible teaches that all men are reasonable, if they are approached properly.

15. (T or F) Reproof is never the cause of enmity.

16. Thought question: How can enemies sometimes be a blessing in disguise?

VI
The Problem of Friends

I. INTRODUCTION

THE normal life is one of friendship. Friends are a reflection of our own worthiness and a source of help for our own inadequacies. Friends are precious responsibilities; therefore, I have the problems of choosing friends, of making and holding friends, and of being a friend.

A friend is like bread for a hungry appetite; like a balancing pole for walking the tight-rope of life; like a soothing ointment for the cuts and bruises of life; like a golden link in the chain of life; and like a vine that clings to us despite our weaknesses.

What one lacks another possesses. We all possess some things in common, but we all are not endowed alike. We find strength in others for our weaknesses, and they find help in us for their failings. This is what makes friendship so delightful.

> There's happiness in little things,
> There's joy in passing pleasure.
> But friendships are, from year to year
> The best of all life's treasure.

II. SELECTING FRIENDS

Solomon made it plain that we should be careful in the selection of friends: "Make no friendship with an angry man; and with a furious man shalt thou not go" (Prov. 22:24).

Then in the next verse he told us why: "Lest thou learn his ways, and get a snare to thy soul" (Prov. 22:25).

Thus it is evident that our selection of friends should not be based upon their wealth, education or prestige, but rather upon their being the right kind of people, regardless of their status in life.

The qualities needed to make and hold friends are also the very qualities to look for in selecting friends.

III. MAKING AND HOLDING FRIENDS

One of the everyday problems of the Christian is to make and hold friends. Thus we need to give thought to doing the things which will attract more friends and keep the ones we have, specifically:

1. *Be friendly.* Solomon said, "A man that hath friends must show himself friendly" (Prov. 18:24). Friendliness is a quality of Christianity; sourness is not. John Wesley said, "Sour godliness is the devil's religion." Warmness draws people; coldness repels them.

Even a dog, without reading books, knows how to make friends and influence people . . . by just being friendly.

Bobby Burns, the National Poet of Scotland, while visiting in a strange city, was very lonely and melancholy. Seeking companionship, he visited a church where he received neither a hand of welcome nor a word of friendship. Before leaving he wrote this verse on the flyleaf of a hymnal:

> As cauld a wind as ever blew;
> A caulder kirk, and in't but few;
> As cauld a minister's e'er spak;
> Ye'll all be hct ere I come back.

Here is a question for each of us: "If I had been in the audience, would it have been any different?"

2. *Be helpful in adversity.* "A friend loveth at all times, and a brother is born for adversity" (Prov. 17:17). That is what a friend is for — born for adversity. You cannot get and retain friends with bare compliments. They are drawn and held by giving them tokens of your love, which in reality are tokens of yourself. In the adverse circumstances of the man who was robbed and wounded, which one made a friend, the priest, the Levite or the Samaritan? (Lk. 10:30-37). You know: the Good Samaritan. And you know why: He was "a brother born for adversity" who extended a helping hand.

There are several good things about adversity, one of which is that it will show you who your real friends are. Adversity is society's laboratory where many a misnamed friendship is proved to be only an acquaintanceship. There are many people who are good at being a friend until you need a friend. They are like a shadow which walks by your side in sunshine but disappears when the clouds come.

3. *Possess a humility that will cause you to mix and mingle with all classes of people.* Social, intellectual or financial snobbery will not make or hold friends. "In lowliness of mind let each esteem other better than" himself (Phil. 2:3) is a good way to make friends. We never look up to the person who is stuck up. We can get down among the people without getting down on their level of sin. Jesus could. He associated with all classes of people, including sinners and publicans (Matt. 9:11). Our Lord never pulled back from sinners, feeling that he was too good to touch them or to be touched by them. He permitted a sinful woman to fall before him and bathe his feet with her tears and dry them with the hair of her head (Lk. 7:36-48). If this were to happen to some church members today, they would be horrified and embarrassed, feeling that they had been disgraced for life.

What some people evidently have not learned is: "Pride goeth before destruction and a haughty spirit before a fall" (Prov. 16:18).

4. *Be unselfish.* "Look not every man on his own things, but every man also on the things of others" (Phil. 2:4) — another good way to win friends. "Even as the Son of man came not to be ministered unto, but to minister, and to give his life a ransom for many" (Matt. 20:28). Some people are too self-centered ever to have many friends. They get up in the morning with this attitude: "Let's see — just what can some of my friends do today to make me happy?" They seem to think "justice" is spelled "just us." There was the childless couple whose prayer was:

> Lord, bless us two
> And that will do.

And an old bachelor is supposed to have prayed:

> Lord, bless only me,
> That's as far as I can see.

Questions: (1) Though I am not guilty of praying such words, am I guilty of practicing such deeds? (2) Are there any good things I am refusing to do for others because of selfishness? (3) What victories have I recently won over selfishness?

5. *Be tolerant.* "Forbearing one another" (Col. 3:13) — a divine injunction. Tolerance is a beautiful and attractive quality to cultivate within ourselves, and as we cultivate ourselves we cultivate our friendships.

If I want others to be tolerant and withhold judgment of me, then I must not judge them. "Judge not, that ye be not judged" (Matt. 7:1). Years of experience have taught us that we are less likely to have the facts than we think, let alone a knowledge of the extenuating circumstances. Each would be less censorious, if he had to walk in the other fellow's moccasins.

One thing that will help us to be more tolerant is to take a look at our own weaknesses. "And why beholdest thou the mote that is in thy brother's eye, but considerest not the beam that is in thine own eye?" (Matt. 7:3).

> Forbear to judge, for we are sinners all.
> Close up his eyes and draw the curtain close;
> And let us all to meditation.
>
> — Shakespeare

6. *Be sincere, truthful and honest.* This is good advice not only in winning friends, but also in business and in just plain living. It must be good because God gave it: "That ye may approve things that are excellent; that ye may be sincere" (Phil 1:10). "Let us walk honestly" (Rom. 13:13).

One of the most ignoble traits of the Pharisees was their insincerity. Jesus said, "They say, and do not" (Matt. 23:3). Then he advised them to clean up first on the inside that the outside of them be clean (Matt. 23:26). So true and lasting friendship with the Lord or anyone else is something that begins on the inside of a person.

Friendship must be natural and spontaneous. It must come like the opening of a fragrant flower in the radiant sunshine. It cannot be forced.

Insincerity will repel would-be friends. We want a friend in whom we can put confidence and trust. He feels the same way about us. Did you ever hear it said, "I don't trust him. He's too oily for me"? Confidence is a prerequisite to trustfulness, and trustfulness is a prerequisite to friendship.

7. *Follow Golden Rule.* "Therefore all things whatso-

ever ye would that men should do to you, do ye even so to them" (Matt. 7:12). There is no better rule for making friends than this. It will not alienate people to treat them as you wish to be treated. This will make you sympathetic, kind and helpful. This will deter you from imposing on them and taking advantage of them.

One lady said, "I used to admire Ruth and expected that we should be good friends, but she's borrowed so many things and never repaid them that I've decided I don't want anyone for a friend who takes such liberties."

8. *Be stable.* Stability will adorn your character and make you inviting as a friend, for the simple reason you will be a source of strength and security to others. No friendship can be any stronger than the persons involved. Each person should "be like a tree planted by the rivers of water, that bringeth forth his fruit in his season; his leaf also shall not wither" (Psa. 1:3). That is the way friendship is. It grows in the rich soil of understanding, watered by the flowing river of love. Its roots have grown deep in human hearts. The leaves do not wither, for this friendship-tree is equal to any heat wave beamed upon it. It brings forth the fruit of helpfulness.

Some people are too deficient in character ever to be anyone's friend. "A double-minded man is unstable in all his ways" (Jas. 1:8) He is like a dog that will hunt with anybody. In trying to be everybody's friend, he becomes nobody's friend. You cannot have a protective friendship with an unstable person; if you try, you will be stabbed in the back when the going gets rough. But the stable person with character will not falter.

> Alter? when the hills do,
> Falter? when the sun
> Question if his glory
> Be the perfect one.

> Surfeit? when the daffodil
> Doth of the dew:
> Even as herself, O friend!
> I will of you!
>
> The Poems of Emily Dickinson
> Published by Little, Brown & Co., Boston

9. *Be loyal.* One thing that gave Paul strength and courage when he was a prisoner in Rome was the loyalty of his friend Onesiphorus. Here is his record of appreciation: "The Lord give mercy unto the house of Onesiphorus; for he oft refreshed me, and was not ashamed of my chain" (II Tim. 1:16). "Not ashamed of my chain" — that was loyalty.

One of the things that hurt poor Job was the disloyalty of supposed friends. He vocalized the hurt by saying: "My kinsfolk have failed, and my familiar friends have forgotten me" (Job 19:14). "All my inward friends abhorred me: and they whom I loved are turned against me" (Job 19:19).

Disappointment in a friend comes sometimes because of our unreasonable expectations. If we ever have cause for humiliation and confession because of our own imperfections, surely our friends are equally as human and susceptible to mistakes. Instead of my being ashamed of my friend's imperfection, whatever it is, I should be ashamed of myself for even thinking of being ashamed of him. It is that kind of friendship "that looks on tempests and is never shaken."

> Love is not love
> Which alters when it alteration finds,
> Or bends with the remover to remove:
> O, no! it is an ever fixed mark
> That lcoks on tempests and is never shaken.
>
> — Shakespeare

One day a young preacher came into my office and said, "Look at me. I'm bleeding all over." What he meant was that he had been stabbed in the back by supposed friends. Well, there is not much you can do about Judases, except just not be one.

10. Summed up, *be a friend.* All of the aforementioned points will make me a friend; and as I become one, others will respond and become my friends.

Personal question: If I were someone else, would I want me as a friend?

REVIEW EXERCISE

1. With whom did Solomon say that we should not make a friendship? ....
2. Why did Solomon warn against the wrong friendship? ....
3. To what extent does a friend love? ....
4. Quote the Golden Rule. ....
5. Of what was Onesiphorus not ashamed? ....
6. How had some supposed friends treated Job? ....
7. For what is a brother born? ....
8. "A man that hath friends must .... himself ...."
   Scripture: ....
9. "In lowliness of .... let each .... other .... than themselves."
10. "Pride goeth before .... and a .... spirit before a fall." Scripture: ....

THE PROBLEM OF FRIENDS

11. List nine qualities essential to friendship. ....
....
....

12. Jesus described the insincerity of the Pharisees by saying, "They say, and ...." Scripture: ....

13. (T or F) Christians are to be forbearing.

14. (T or F) Jesus came to be ministered unto.

15. (T or F) A double-minded man is unstable.

16. Thought question: What practical things can I do to win more friends?

VII
The Problem of Time

I. INTRODUCTION

TIME has always been a problem for man, because he has only a limited amount of it. The scarcity and uncertainty of the world's most precious and irreplaceable commodity place a tremendous and grave responsibility upon the Christian for the way he uses it.

Our days are few and wrought with trouble. "Man that is born of a woman is of few days and full of trouble" (Job 14:1,2). Few days which are trouble-filled — this presents some problems.

II. PROBLEMS RELATIVE TO TIME

1. *I have the problem of learning my frailty and the measure of my days.* I know it and yet I don't know it. I know life is short for the other fellow, but I am inclined to think that time will tarry with me. So I must learn and apply the lesson to myself.

Life is something we live daily; so man's frailty is a daily problem. In solving it, I need to take the matter to God in prayer and ask for his help, as did the Psalmist: "Lord, make me to know mine end, and the measure of my days, what it is; that I may know how frail I am" (Psa. 39:4). "So teach us to number our days, that we may apply our hearts unto wisdom" (Psa: 90:12). If we learn this, we shall be smart.

2. *I have the everyday problem of protecting my body*

and caring for my health to the end that my days may be lengthened. "The days of our years are threescore years and ten; and if by reason of strength they be fourscore years, yet is their strength labor and sorrow; for it is soon cut off, and we fly away" (Psa. 90:10). By reason of strength, man's years may be increased. So man is daily duty-bound to eat nutritiously, sleep adequately, work sensibly, exercise sufficiently and relax restfully. Whatever contributes to my longevity is a daily problem; and I must realize it; and I must do something about it. Neither life nor time is to be taken lightly.

3. *I have the problem of redeeming time.* The Holy Spirit says, "Redeeming the time, because the days are evil" (Eph. 5:16). Redeem means to buy back. We have already wasted too much time; therefore, we need to buy back all of it we can.

Idleness is not for the Christian. The householder in the parable asked, "Why stand ye here all the day idle?" (Matt. 20:6). One problem, if not solved correctly, leads to others. So the sin of idleness fathers many more sins. "And withal they learn to be idle, wandering about from house to house; and not only idle, but tattlers also and busybodies, speaking things which they ought not" (I Tim. 5:13).

As you see, idleness may get to be a deadly peril. You have heard it said, "The trouble with Mrs. Busybody is she just has too much spare time on her hands"; and "Oh, if Miss Tattler had more work to do and less time to talk."

4. *I have to daily face the temptation of procrastinating until tomorrow to do what should be done today.* The great words of the Bible are "now" and "today." "Now is the accepted time" (II Cor. 6:2). "Today if ye will hear his voice" (Heb. 3:7,8).

Tomorrow is in the realm of the unknown. Solomon

said, "Boast not thyself of tomorrow; for thou knowest not what a day may bring forth" (Prov. 27:1). Tomorrow may bring sickness, incapacitation or death; or even though health favors you, tomorrow there may be decreased interest, faded desire or shattered faith.

Tomorrow is the fool's day. Jesus called one man a fool, because he planned big things tomorrow at the expense of neglecting his soul today (Lk. 12:16-21). That will make one a fool. All that tomorrow meant to him was death. Whatever intentions he may have had for self-improvement and world-betterment died with him. On his tomb they could have inscribed the epitaph: TOMORROW.

> Tomorrow, and tomorrow, and tomorrow
> Creeps in this petty pace from day to day,
> To the last syllable of recorded time;
> And all our yesterdays have lighted fools
> The way to dusty death.
>
> — *Macbeth*, Shakespeare

Now let us do a little soul-searching about this problem of tomorrow:

(1) What about the letter I was going to write Tom and Mary tomorrow? Now it has been so long I am ashamed to write.

(2) And what about the thank-you note I was going to write tomorrow to Sue? She had been so thoughtful of me. Oh, how time flies — it has been six months.

(3) What ever happened to that tomorrow I was going to begin reading the Bible everyday?

(4) And what about that tomorrow I was going to visit grandmother? She will not be with us long.

(5) What about my saying I would visit Henry in the

hospital tomorrow? He is now well, but when he needed me I let tomorrow stand between us.

(6) Then there was the tomorrow I was going to visit the new family that moved in down the street and invite them to church. They are no longer new. It has been a year, and I have never met them.

(7) And there was that tomorrow I was especially saving to begin attending Sunday evening services. The years have passed and I am still just a Sunday morning attender.

(8) And what about that tomorrow I was going to apologize to Pearl for the wrong I had done her? Now what was once no more than an ant hill has become a towering mountain.

(9) That bad habit was going to be broken tomorrow, but that tomorrow has never come and the habit is stronger than ever.

(10) Tomorrow I was going to be a light in this old world; but because it takes effort to keep oil in the bowl and the globe shined, I have waited for a day to come which seldom ever comes — tomorrow.

> He was going to be all that a mortal should be Tomorrow.
> No one would be better than he Tomorrow.
> Each morning he stacked up the letters he'd write Tomorrow.
> It was too bad indeed he was too busy to see Bill,
>   but he promised to do it Tomorrow.
>
> The greatest of workers this man would have been Tomorrow.
> The world would have known him had he ever seen Tomorrow.
> But the fact is he died and faded from view, and all that
>   was left when living was through
> Was a mountain of things he intended to do Tomorrow.

III. OTHERS HAVE HAD THE PROBLEM OF TIME

1. *The problem of time was one of the major problems*

Felix failed to overcome. Paul preached to him of "righteousness, temperance, and judgment to come" (Acts 24:25). The Word had such effect that Felix trembled, but he lost the battle of time. He said, "Go thy way for this time; when I have a convenient season, I will call for thee" (Acts 24:25). He waited for the convenient season. It did not come.

2. *The foolish virgins* were good women, but they failed to solve the problem of time (Matt. 25:1-12). They were in the kingdom and they wanted to meet the bridegroom and they had made some preparation, but not enough. The spirit of tomorrow was the cause of their ruin. They went forth to make more preparation, but it was too late. Time ran out on them.

IV. WASTING TIME

We can save time by not wasting it. There are many ways time is wasted:

1. *Lack of application.* If we accomplish things, we must apply ourselves. Solomon said, "Whatsoever thy hand findeth to do, do it with thy might" (Eccl. 9:10). Because play is easier and more fun, the child refuses to apply himself very long. But we are adults and as such should put away childish traits. Paul said, "When I became a man, I put away childish things" (I Cor. 13:11). So acting my age is a problem.

2. *Reading cheap literature.* The country is filled with demoralizing literature. Some is vulgar. Some is suggestive. Some is propaganda. What a waste of time and talent, paper and ink. As one reads he thinks. My duty as a Christian is to think on the higher and nobler things (Phil. 4:8). I can save my mind from evil thoughts by keeping it filled with good thoughts.

3. *Unwholesome recreation.* The world is pleasure-mad, and is wasting time in the dizzy pursuit of the same. "Lovers of pleasure more than lovers of God" (II Tim. 3:4). And most of their pleasures are only mirages . . . look like they would quench their thirst but turn out to be only dried sand in the throat. Everyone needs recreation, but let's be sure it recreates. If it tears me down physically, mentally, morally or spiritually, it is not recreation; it is dissipation.

4. *Meditating on fanciful injuries* is a very hurtful way to waste time. Carrying chips on the shoulder takes both strength and time that could be used constructively. Even though the wrong is real rather than imaginary, meditating upon it will bring only bitterness and frustration. Forget it. Leave it to the Lord. "Vengeance is mine; I will repay, saith the Lord" (Rom. 12:19).

5. *Pondering past mistakes.* No accountable being is perfect. Every life has its own weaknesses. Great men have made great mistakes. Paul declared that he had been the chief of sinners, but he obtained pardon from a merciful God and put his past sins behind him. He declared, "Forgetting those things which are behind, and reaching forth unto those things which are before" (Phil. 3:13). When God forgives sin, he forgets it (Heb. 8:12), and so should we. If we get bogged down in the past, we can never go forward.

6. *Many people waste time worrying about what may happen in the future.* We need the faith to accept the promise that God will work out all things for our good (Rom. 8:28). We do not know the future, but we know God is in it and this should suffice to quiet our nerves. Here are three time-saving rules:

(1) Turn loose of yesterday for it is gone.

(2) Do not reach for tomorrow for it has not come.

(3) Grab today for it is here.

7. *Gossiping or lending ears to gossipers* is a sinful way to squander time. God has said, "Thou shalt not go up and down as a talebearer among thy people" (Lev. 19:16). What evil! What waste of time! We have lived long enough to know that 95% of all hurtful rumors are false. In playing gossip at parties, you learned that anything which is repeated three or four times cannot be recognized. Even if the story you repeat or to which you give your ears should be true, it is both a loss of time and injurious if it hurts someone. Wounds for another! "The words of a talebearer are as wounds" (Prov. 26:22). So one way I can solve the problem of time is by refusing to be a party to gossip, by speaking it or by hearing it.

8. *Some waste time by lying in bed* longer than is needful or helpful. "Love not sleep, lest thou come to poverty" (Prov. 20:13). We need both rest and work and should keep the two in proper proportion.

9. *Another devastation of time is unusually long telephone conversations.* I knew a man who would argue with you that the telephone is an instrument of the devil. He had a point, even though I disagree. It can also be an instrument of God. However, anyone can use it to invade your privacy whenever he wishes and hold you longer than you desire. It is an act of courtesy for me to state my business and get through. A little bit of the Golden Rule helps here.

10. *Many people kill time by crucifying it on the cross of disorganization.* Every day they haphazardly run the gamut from "A to Z" and from "Dan to Beersheba," without spending enough time on any one thing to get a job

done. If I would save time, I must get my work organized.

11. *Time is also wasted through slow movements.* Paul once sent word to Silas and Timothy "to come to him with all speed" (Acts 17:15).

Lincoln was known for many qualities, one of which was his wit. On one occasion he rented a horse and buggy to go to a town where he was scheduled to make a political speech. The opposition conspired for him to get the slowest horse in the livery, thinking he would be too late for the speech. When Lincoln returned he said to the livery man, "I suppose you keep this horse for funerals." "No, no," replied the owner. Lincoln continued, "Well, I'm glad to hear that; for if you did, the chances are you wouldn't get the corpse to the cemetery in time for the resurrection."

I can save time by moving faster, provided I do it advisedly.

12. *Hesitancy in making decisions will steal our time.* It keeps one in a quandary. It is like being on a merry-go-round. We are against hasty decisions, but dragging out the decision is not good either. The person who can never make up his mind is always lagging behind. I must get the facts, weigh the facts and then reach my decision.

REVIEW EXERCISE

1. Why did the Psalmist wish to number his days? ....

....

2. What question is asked in the Bible concerning idleness? ....

....

3. What sins does Paul link with idleness? ....

....

4. Why did Jesus call the rich man in Luke 12 a fool? ....
   ....

5. What was Felix's mistake? ....

6. What was the mistake of the foolish virgins? ....
   ....

7. How can we save time by forgetting? ....
   ....

8. Man's days are .... and .... trouble.

9. "The days of our years are .... years and ....;
   and if by reason of .... they be ....
   years." Scripture: ....

10. "Boast not thyself of ...." Why? ....
    ....

11. Quote the passage which teaches we should apply ourselves to
    our work. ....
    ....

12. Some people lose time by loving .... more than ....
    Scripture: ....

13. (T or F) The Psalmist prayed to know how frail he was.

14. (T & F) The Bible teaches that we should buy back time.

15. (T or F) Paul said we should remember our mistakes and reach for the things which are before.

16. Thought question: If I had only one year to live, how would I spend it?

VIII
The Problem of Employment

I. INTRODUCTION

ONE of my daily problems is to make a living. To do this, I must be either self-employed or employed by others or have annuities and savings accumulated from past labors. With most of us there is the necessary problem of labor; but without it, there are more stressing problems. So what is considered a problem with its many facets is actually our friend and preserver.

II. THE NECESSITY OF LABOR

1. *From man's beginning in the garden of Eden, God has appointed labor as a necessary part of man's life.* "And the Lord God took the man, and put him into the garden of Eden to dress it and to keep it" (Gen. 2:15). God could have fed man without this, but he knew what was best for man. Thus Eden was a paradise of work.

2. *After the downfall of man, the law of labor was renewed.* God said to man, "In the sweat of thy face shalt thou eat bread, till thou return unto the ground" (Gen. 3:19); but now in a world of multiplying thorns and thistles.

3. *Solomon used the ant as an object to teach us the urgency of labor* (Prov. 6:6-8). All nature is at work.

4. *This law of labor is so fixed that God says it is either work or starve.* Paul expressed it: "For even when we were with you, this we commanded you, that if any would

not work, neither should he eat" (II Thess. 3:10). Of course, a few can circumvent this law by parasitically living off the fruits of others; but not all can do this, for somebody must work.

The best way to fight poverty is to go to work. It is a fact which has no exceptions that we must labor for all we have, and nothing is worth having that costs us nothing. The cat likes the fish, but not enough to do the wading. We like gold, but dread the digging.

5. *Even our Lord toiled while here on earth.* His occupation was carpentry. It was hard for men to reconcile his mighty works with his trade, and thus they asked: "Is not this the carpenter, the son of Mary . . .?" (Mk. 6:3).

6. *There must be royalty in work, for God worked.* He worked six days before he rested on the seventh (Gen. 2:2).

7. *God who worked has so arranged the laws of nature for us to be his fellow workers.* Through the centuries man has had to do his share of work to have the blessings of God. The trees stand as monuments to God's work, but man must cut and saw them to have a house. The water is a wondrous work of God, but it is man's work to dam up the rivers and dig the wells. In this way, man works with God to house, feed and clothe man. As you go forth each day to do what seems like a little drudgery, you will find inspiration and strength in realizing that you are God's fellow helper. You will have a better job, if you take a better view of it.

In George Eliot's expressive poem on the famous violin-maker, Antonio Stradivari, we have a classical tribute to man's partnership in work with God.

Not God Himself can make man's best
Without best men to help him.
'Tis God gives skill,
But not without man's hands: He could not make
Antonio Stradivari's violins without Antonio.

III. MAN NEEDS EMPLOYMENT FOR HIS OWN GOOD

As already discussed, man needs employment for a living, but also for other essential reasons:

1. *Man needs employment for the strength of his mind and body.* An unused muscle remains undeveloped and withers into helplessness. Put that muscle into action and it firms and hardens like a steel spring. Every muscle, nerve, and mental and moral faculty follows the same law. Physical activity develops the body, study stimulates the brain, and adherence to moral principles strengthens man's inner nature.

2. *Man needs to work, for it is work that helps to make the man.* While toiling at our work, our work is toiling at us. While the farmer cultivates the crop, the crop cultivates the farmer. And as a man builds a house, the house builds the man. The same kind of work he puts into a visible house outside himself goes into an invisible house that rises within himself. If into one he puts dishonesty and rotten materials, into the other goes proportionate amounts of the same. So in doing our work, we are actually doing ourselves. Our Lord stated the principle in this manner: "Even so every good tree bringeth forth good fruit; but a corrupt tree bringeth forth evil fruit" (Matt. 7:17).

3. *You can never enjoy the sweetness of rest and sleep until you have tasted the bitterness of rigorous toil.* Solomon said, "The sleep of a laboring man is sweet" (Eccl. 5:12). It is true of the cotton picker who works from dawn

to dawn, the harvest hand who toils from "can" to "can't," and the school teacher who props his eyelids open with another cup of coffee and keeps on grading papers. Sleep can be so sweet, if work has been so strenuous.

4. *If man is not busy in constructive works, idleness may enslave him to destructive deeds.* This was true in the Thessalonian church. Paul wrote, "For we hear that there are some which walk among you disorderly, working not at all, but are busybodies" (II Thess. 3:11). They were not busy — they were busybodies. The busybody is classified with murderers, thieves and other evildoers (I Pet. 4:15).

We have seen retired people blight their closing days with gossip, slander, hate, strife and calumny. Of course, they had a heart for such all time, but a busy schedule had saved them from much of it. We have seen others with different hearts who, when they retired, busied themselves in doing more good than ever. Able-bodied persons are not likely to sit with time on their hands. They are more apt to do something, good or bad. So whether you are employed or retired, there are plenty of good works to which you may give yourself.

We thank God for work, for what we need is work to do and strength to do it.

> Upon thy bended knees, thank God for work!
> In workless days all ills and evils lurk,
> For work to do, and strength to do the work,
> We thank Thee, Lord!
> — John Oxenham

5. *Employment of the mind in some manner is essential to happiness.* Idleness is the mother of misery. It is the man of leisure who mopes and imagines himself in a madhouse or a grave. There are many well-meaning people

who will kill you by having you to rest yourself to death. Work does not shorten life, but worry does. Employment is nature's physician. It is friction rather than motion that destroys the machinery. Here is a worry preventive: "Trust in the Lord with all thine heart; and lean not unto thine own understanding" (Prov. 3:5).

6. *We must be employed to keep from wasting life.* If we waste time, we waste life. We have already wasted too much time or life. We need to redeem or buy back all of it we can. "Redeeming the time, because the days are evil" (Eph. 5:16).

> Count that day lost whose low descending sun
> Views from thy hand no worthy action done.

IV. THE GOOD WORKER

Some workers are good; some are poor; and some are medium. As Christians we should seek to excel as employees, employers, business owners and executives, and professional men and women. All other things being equal, the Christian should be a better worker than the person of the world. As one becomes a good and worthy worker, he solves many of the problems pertaining to employment; therefore, it is highly appropriate that we note the following traits:

1. *The good worker sees not only what he does, but what it does for others.* If I do this, then that which otherwise would be drudgery will be a gratifying experience. I should see my little labor as a necessary part of the world's work. The farmer who works hard with soiled hands should see not only a field of wheat, but the many families sitting around tables eating bread made from that wheat. The carpenter should see not only houses, but the people sheltered and protected by them. This enhances the worker's feelings of accomplishment.

2. *The good worker is enthusiastic.* "Whatsoever thy hand findeth to do, do it with thy might" (Eccl. 9:10). When a man puts his whole soul into his work, he makes it a job worth while. A banker friend of mine once said, "There can be no substitute for brains; but if there could be, it would be enthusiasm."

3. *The excellent worker looks on his work as a sacred charge to do his best at it.* All poor work is a fraud and a lie. "Thou knowest the commandments . . . Defraud not . . ." (Mk. 10:19).

4. *The most meritorious worker is happy in his employment.* If you cannot be pleased with your job, find another one. It wrongs both you and your employer to remain on a job you dislike.

A personnel man put the question to one hundred men, "How many of you fellows are thoroughly satisfied with your job?" Only five hands went up. "What's the matter?" "Not enough money," one answered. Another replied, "I'm not interested in this kind of work." Another stated, "I took this job until something better comes along."

It has been estimated that seventy per cent of American labor is not producing more than fifty per cent of its capacity. So lots of people are being overpaid while they whine for better jobs.

Paul said, "For I have learned, in whatsoever state I am, therewith to be content" (Phil. 4:11). When the need arose, he made tents (Acts 18:3).

You may turn work into play by working at the thing you love or for those you love. Liking your employment is not wholly dependent on the job, but on self and self-discipline.

> It is not doing the thing we like,
> but liking the thing we have to do
> that makes life happy.
>
> — Goethe

5. *The worthy worker is a diligent worker.* "He becometh poor that dealeth with a slack hand: but the hand of the diligent maketh rich" (Prov. 10:4).

The slothful man can never succeed. When duty beckons he says, "There is a lion without, I shall be slain in the streets" (Prov. 22:13). He always has an excuse.

Dan and Sam were two brothers whose farms lay side by side. In the spring Dan said, "The weeds are coming, but weeds as well as grain are part of the Creator's plan; so we must be resigned." And he lay down for his usual afternoon doze.

Sam said, "I can be resigned only to what I cannot help." So he went to work and ploughed and hoed until his fields were cleared of weeds.

You know the results. Sam prospered and Dan didn't. The years broadened the differences between the two. Dan said, "Why are you always prospering, but I am not? Everything you do succeeds, while everything I do fails."

He didn't know that to pull ahead, you must use your head. He didn't know that the trouble with success is it takes work. He didn't know the "Man of the Hour" never watches the clock. He didn't know that while the successful man tips his hat to past accomplishments, he takes off his coat to present duties.

6. *The good worker is honest.* This is one of the most necessary qualities. God's plan for success requires honesty. "Provide things honest in the sight of all men" (Rom. 12:17). "Thou shalt not steal" (Ex. 20:15).

Work to have to give to others — not work to steal from others (Eph. 4:28).

The old rugged quality of honesty would solve many of our problems in the economic world. Every employee should realize that for him to take pay for services not rendered is theft. One thing we all can be is honest.

7. *The excellent worker is productive.* There will always be a demand for the worker who produces, but the non-productive worker hinders success and, sooner or later, must be eliminated. Jesus exemplified this principle. "And when he saw a fig tree in the way, he came to it, and found nothing thereon, but leaves only, and said unto it, Let no fruit grow on thee henceforward for ever. And presently the fig tree withered away" (Matt. 21:19). There is no need to have a fig tree that does not bear. Neither is there any need for a worker that does not produce.

8. *The good worker works his mind to improve his work.* There will always be a place for the person who does this. So often we see placards which say, "THINK." We think about what interests us. If we have enough interest in our job, we shall give thought to how we may improve it.

WHY HE FAILS

There's many an industrious man
  Who never gets ahead,
Because he does not think or plan,
  But trusts to luck instead.
He's not a slacker or a shirk,
  This plodder in life's grind;
But though he always minds his work,
  He never works his mind.

The good worker is like a good watch: open face, busy hands, pure gold, well regulated and wound up.

THE PROBLEM OF EMPLOYMENT

REVIEW EXERCISE

1. When was man first commanded to work? ....
2. What is sweet to a laboring man? ....
3. What are we commanded to redeem? ....
4. What is the fate of him that deals with a slack hand?.................... ....
5. What excuse does the slothful man give for not working?............ ....
6. What lesson did Jesus teach in smiting the fig tree?...................... ....
7. What living thing did Solomon use to teach us the urgency of work? ....
8. "Some which walk among you disorderly .... not at all, but are ...." Scripture: ....
9. "Whatsoever thy .... findeth to do, do it with thy ...." Scripture: ....
10. "Provide things .... in the sight of all men." Scripture: ....
11. There is royalty in work because ....
12. "The hand of the .... maketh rich." Scripture: ....
13. (T or F) It is God's will that if any would not work, neither should he eat.
14. (T or F) Paul as a preacher never did any material work.
15. (T or F) Jesus had a trade.
16. Thought question: Why is it that while man toils at his work, his work toils at him?

IX
The Problem of Individual Leadership

I. INTRODUCTION

THERE is the leadership of elders, deacons, teachers and various committees, but there is also the leadership of the individual. My chief problem is with myself. What others may or may not do in the realm of leadership will not solve my problem of doing some leading of my own. I must forge ahead regardless of what others may do. While we need capable and enthusiastic group leadership in every congregation, perhaps the more crying need is self-initiated activity.

II. EXAMPLES IN THE BIBLE

1. *Joseph of Arimathea stands out as a noble example of personal leadership.* When Jesus was crucified, his body needed to be lovingly and respectfully buried. There was a need and the rich man, Joseph, filled the need. "He went to Pilate, and begged the body of Jesus." Then he took the body and "wrapped it in a clean linen cloth, and laid it in his own new tomb" (Matt. 27:57-60).

This took foresight, initiative, determination, courage and sacrifice; and Joseph had all of it. It was a tender and loving work of self-reliance. This was not the work of a group. This was not the fulfillment of an assignment given to Joseph by others. Instead, as far as we know, he did it all by himself. It may be that many other disciples also saw what should be done, but let the thought die for lack of leadership. We make our thoughts a reality or let them perish for a lack of initiative.

2. *It was Andrew's individual leadership that directed Simon Peter to Jesus.* After this fisherman enlisted with the Lord, he "first findeth his own brother Simon, and saith unto him, We have found the Messias, which is, being interpreted, the Christ. And he brought him to Jesus" (Jno. 1:41,42). No committee gave Andrew this job. The opportunity did not have to be pointed out to Andrew. Contrariwise, he saw it and he did it.

The Great Commission requires personal leadership in soul winning (Matt. 28:19,20). Each Christian is commanded to go forth and teach others, and the baptized are required to teach others and on and on it goes. Evangelizing the world is too big a task for a few. But the Lord's chain reaction plan will work, and I am a part of the plan. It demands that I exercise the strongest and most effective personal leadership I can muster.

3. *The individual members of the Jerusalem church exerted leadership in spreading the gospel.* A severe and painful persecution scattered them abroad. Chased and pursued, homeless and penniless, strangers and foreigners, they did not forget their calling as Christians. "Therefore they that were scattered abroad went every where preaching the word" (Acts 8:4). They did not preach to live; they lived to preach.

This took leadership and they had it. So evidently if there is enough inward compulsion, the outward manifestations we call initiative will follow. The Bible teaches this: "Then I said, I will not make mention of him, nor speak any more in his name. But his word was in mine heart as a burning fire shut up in my bones, and I was weary with forbearing, and I could not stay" (Jer. 20:8, 9). His word "in mine heart as a burning fire shut up in my bones" will compel me to seek the lost whether I am on a committee or not. When the heart is running over, there is no place for it to go except through the eyes or mouth — tears or words. "For out of the abundance of the heart the mouth speaketh" (Matt. 12:34). This explains the most dynamic and effective program of evangelism the world has ever known. We favor strong leadership within a congregation, but we recognize that the spirit and power that mostly took the gospel to the world in the first century was individual leadership.

4. A couple showed personal leadership in teaching a preacher (Acts 18:24-26) The couple, Aquilla and Priscilla. The preacher, Apollos. "And he began to speak boldly in the synagogue: whom when Aquilla and Priscilla had heard, they took him unto them, and expounded unto him the way of God more perfectly."

This was not a group effort. This was not a project planned by the elders and executed by two of the members, which would have been scriptural. It was rather the work of a couple who saw their duty and did it without consulting flesh and blood.

This was a work which required:

(1) Concern and they manifested it.
(2) Love and they showed it.
(3) Knowledge and they taught it.
(4) Sacrifice and they made it.
(5) Self-reliance and they demonstrated it.
(6) Leadership and they had it.

5. The Good Samaritan individually led in relieving hu-

man suffering (Lk. 10:30-37). A traveler who was going from Jerusalem to Jericho was robbed, wounded and left half dead. A certain priest came by and just looked at him and passed by on the other side. A Levite came and did the same thing. But a certain Samaritan came "and when he saw him, he had compassion on him, and went to him, and bound up his wounds, pouring in oil and wine, and set him on his own beast, and brought him to an inn, and took care of him." That is not all. "On the morrow when he departed, he took out two pence, and gave them to the host, and said unto him, Take care of him: and whatsoever thou spendest more, when I come again, I will repay thee."

The Samaritan was not the footman of some group which requested him to do it. He was not fulfilling an assignment in an organized work; and this, too, would have been good, because human beings need to work with one another and that necessitates leadership, organization and cooperation. What we are saying is: He did it by himself through his own leadership. He obeyed the Golden Rule without asking anybody. There was an opportunity to serve and he seized it.

The paradoxical thing is that the two men who were recognized as "leaders" failed to lead, and the man who was supposed to have no leadership qualities led in demonstrating who a neighbor is. A compassion that would not be stilled made the difference; and while one had it, two did not.

6. *Cornelius led in getting a group together to hear the word of God.* While he waited for Peter to come and preach the truth, he got busy and "called together his kinsmen and near friends" (Acts 10:24). He was successful. Many came. When Peter arrived, Cornelius said, "Now

therefore are we all here present before God, to hear all things that are commanded thee of God" (Acts 10:33).

Why was a large group present? One man's individual leadership brought them together. It was not an act directed by others. He knew that if he needed to hear the words of salvation, others did, too; so he did something about it — that's leadership.

III. OTHER EXAMPLES

1. *The first church ever established in Fort Worth* was the Lord's church and it was the fruit of individual leadership. In the vicinity of the Court House there is a high bluff overlooking the great Trinity River valley to the north. More than a century ago there was only a fort and a few settlers who lived along the rim of the bluff. The valley which is now highly industrialized was then covered with harvest fields. In that early day Brother Dean rode into the village with a pistol in one saddle bag and a Bible in the other. He secured a job as harvest hand. After working hard all day, he would preach at night to the settlers in the settlement. He brought in the sheaves by day and by night. One was physical and the other was spiritual. When the harvest was finished, he mounted his horse and rode away, leaving a little congregation of eight souls, the first in Fort Worth.

This cowboy and harvest hand was not sent here by some congregation to plant the church in Fort Worth, which would have been good. It was the individual work of a man who saw his duty and did it. His standing alone did not deter him. His being tired in body did not stop him. His being short on education did not discourage him. His not being paid made no difference. He saw an opportunity and took advantage of it — that's individual leadership.

2. I was eighteen when I held *my first gospel meeting*

and had been a Christian less than a year. The church did not call me to hold that meeting, for there was no church there. No church sent me to hold it, for no church had shown any interest in that community. I borrowed some song books and benches, put up a sign made of cardboard and painted with crayola. The meeting lasted ten days, at the end of which fourteen had been baptized into Christ and a congregation had been established. I received $6.00 in pay and spent that on expenses. The Lord was my only employer in that meeting, and he has paid me a thousand fold since then.

3. I knew *a Christian farmer in Grayson County, Texas*, whose neighbor became ill. The neighbor's crop began to grow up with grass and weeds. This neighbor was filled with prejudice and would not attend our services. The Christian went over and took his sons and his hired hands and worked out the sick man's crops. As they were working, this sick man, lying on his bed and looking out his window, said to his wife, "You know, when they have their meetin' this summer, we're going to have to go." They did, and they obeyed the gospel. He became very active in the church. A few years passed and he moved to the Northwest. He established a congregation there and later the congregation secured time on radio and preached the gospel to many people hundreds of miles away.

Where did it all begin? Back in the cotton and corn fields of Grayson County, Texas. It began in the big heart of a man who had individual initiative. Neither the preacher nor the elders asked him to do it. He did not have to be asked. He saw a job he could do and did it — that's individual leadership.

IV. PREREQUISITES OF LEADERSHIP

Leadership requires:

1. *You to lead.* Now that is logical. It sounds simple, but it is actually a profound truth.

> You cannot lead where you do not go.
> You cannot tell what you do not know.

The Christian must have the spirit of Paul who said, "Be ye followers of me, even as I also am of Christ" (I Cor. 11:1).

We must not be like the man who prayed at church: "Oh, Lord, use me in thy service, especially in an advisory capacity." It is true that all human beings need advice, but the man who gives it has to say, "Follow me."

2. *Knowledge.* Each Christian is commanded to gain it. "Add to your faith virtue; and to virtue, knowledge" (II Pet. 1:5). We should be ready at all times to give an answer for the hope we have. I should know what I believe and why I believe it. Zeal without knowledge is dangerous, just as knowledge without zeal is useless.

3. *Wisdom* — and certainly enough to know there is a difference between leading and forcing.

A boy scout who was battered and bruised was asked by the scout master what happened. He stated that he had tried to help an old lady across the street. "But what caused you to get hurt?" He replied, "She didn't want to go."

Jesus said that if the people will not hear you (allow you to lead them), then "shake off the dust of your feet" (Matt. 10:14). Do not try to force them. I must remember this, lest I cast pearls before swine (Matt. 7:6) who will trample the pearls and turn again and rend me.

4. *Conviction.* "I believed, and therefore I have spoken" (II Cor. 4:13). Strong faith produced individual leadership. Great leaders have always been men and women with great convictions. Strong faith makes strong people.

5. *Vision.* If I lead, I must have the ability to see what needs to be done. This is not only a prerequisite to leadership, but is also a necessary requirement of survival. "Where there is no vision, the people perish" (Prov. 29:18).

6. *Sacrifice.* I cannot lead others without paying a price. It takes time, effort and energy. The Christian is commanded to present his body a living sacrifice (Rom. 12:1).

7. *Courage.* It takes courage to push ahead. Fear, over-caution, has been the cause of many a defeat. It keeps the crops from being planted in the spring or unharvested in the fall. "He that observeth the wind shall not sow; and he that regardeth the clouds shall not reap" (Eccl. 11:4).

> Do not despair of life. You have no doubt force enough to overcome your obstacles. Think of the fox prowling through wood and field in a winter night for something to satisfy his hunger. Notwithstanding cold and hounds and traps, his race survives. I do not believe any of them ever committed suicide.
> — Thoreau

Great leaders have been fearless men and women.

> O for a man who is a man, and, as my neighbor says, has a bone in his back which you cannot pass your hand through.
> — Thoreau

8. *A tough skin.* He who leads must be able to take criticism, most of which will be destructive and unjust. If you lead the band, you must face the music. The greater the leader, the greater the criticism; so it may be a compliment to be criticized. It does not make you evil for evil people to criticize you. You will be criticized whether you do right or wrong; so be sure you are right and go ahead. "For it is better, if the will of God be so, that ye suffer for well doing, than for evildoing" (I Pet. 3:17).

THE CHRISTIAN'S EVERYDAY PROBLEMS

REVIEW EXERCISE

1. What individual leadership did Joseph of Arimathea exercise? ....

2. What did the Jerusalem Christians do when they were scattered abroad? ....
....

3. What reaction did Jeremiah suffer when he tried to refrain from mentioning the Lord? ....
....

4. What great work of individual leadership did the Good Samaritan perform? ....
....
....

5. Why did Cornelius call together his kinsmen and near friends? ....

6. On what condition did Paul ask others to follow him? ....
....

7. What are we commanded to do when people refuse to hear us? ....

8. What is the fate of those who have no vision? ....

9. "For out of the abundance of the .... the .... speaketh." Scripture: ....

10. Give the names of a couple who showed individual leadership in teaching a preacher. ....

11. "I believed, and therefore I have ...." Scripture:................

THE PROBLEM OF INDIVIDUAL LEADERSHIP 89

12. Quote the passage which shows that over-caution can defeat us.

    ....

    ....

13. (T or F) Whether you do well or evil, you will suffer criticism.

14. (T or F) Simon Peter through his own study found the way of the Lord.

15. (T or F) Joseph, a rich man, once begged.

16. Thought question: What am I doing in individual leadership to further the Lord's cause?

X
The Problem of Contrary Winds

I. INTRODUCTION

"AND he saw them toiling in rowing; for the wind was contrary unto them" (Mk. 6:48). This was an actual experience of the early disciples on a literal sea. Reverse winds necessitated more "toiling in rowing." God knows best. He gave us the winds for the distribution of heat and rainfall. If the heat which comes from the sun stayed where it fell, the equatorial region would be too hot for life and the northern region would be locked in eternal frost.

We cannot have the winds, however, without having them sometimes for us and sometimes against us, but this keeps life from being dull and boresome. Change makes life more interesting and struggle makes man stronger. In countries where the least effort is required for man's survival, he has had the least initiative, lowest ambition and made the slightest progress. Advantage proved to be disadvantage and easy living became a hard way of life.

II. WE HAVE TO ROW AGAINST CONTRARY WINDS

The incident in the text suggests an interesting analogy in our voyage through life.

1. *Man still has to battle contrary winds.* Our world is one of exertion and struggle. Man must face the elements in the material world and wrestle with the forces of evil in the moral and spiritual world. God does not lay restraint upon the winds, but rather permits them to blow

against us — at times he quiets the winds in a brief cessation from the storm lest man be overcome, but not as a permanent protection for man.

2. *There is no escape from opposing winds by simply becoming a Christian.* The children of God in all ages have had to face them. The winds of hate, misrepresentation, betrayal, persecution and miscalculated plans have blown against them with terrific fury. In fact, the winds have always seemed contrary to everyone who has had an earnest and high purpose in life, including the greats like Joseph and Paul.

(1) Joseph was sold into slavery by envious, hateful brothers (Gen. 37:28) — things seemed to be going wrong. Then as a slave he saw his good name ruined and his spotless reputation smeared by a lying, conniving woman who sought to get even with him for his refusal to become her secret love partner (Gen. 39:7-20) — everything seemed to be getting worse. But God was preparing him and lifting him to a higher and nobler work as the food administrator and the second highest official in the Egyptian kingdom (Gen. 41:38-41). Opposing winds were driving Joseph in the right direction — he just did not know it at the time.

(2) Paul, an apostle, had to battle discouraging forces all his Christian life (II Cor. 11:24-27). Problems! Problems! Paul had them. Contrary winds — how they did blow; and it required much "toiling in rowing," but his voyage on life's tempestuous sea was a success. The unconquerable hero victoriously declared, "The things which happened unto me have fallen out rather unto the furtherance of the gospel" (Phil. 1:12). They finally put him to death; but in his losing, he won; and in his dying, he lives.

3. *Adverse winds discipline us.* By having plans go

wrong, we learn to be more humble and more dependent upon God. Unrealized aims teach us to say, "If the Lord will, we shall live, and do this, or that" (Jas. 4:15). We learn to put the trust where it belongs.

God knows we need the chastisement. Though it is grievous at the time, it is for our good. "Now no chastening for the present seemeth to be joyous, but grievous: nevertheless afterward it yieldeth the peaceable fruit of righteousness unto them which are exercised thereby" (Heb. 12:11).

4. *Negative circumstances try man's faith.* "By faith Abraham, when he was tried, offered up Isaac: and he that had received the promises offered up his only begotten son" (Heb. 11:17). It seemed to be an opposing command that required Abraham to offer his son on the altar. But he laid his son on the altar and "stretched forth his hand and took the knife to slay" him. It was then that God stayed his hand and said, "Now I know that thou fearest God" (Gen. 22:12).

5. *Opposing winds provide an opportunity for our greatness (if we have it) to shine as gold.* Job is an inspiring example. He was "perfect and upright, and one that feared God, and eschewed evil . . . the greatest of all the men of the east" (Job. 1:1-4). On a certain day his cattle were stolen by the Sabeans; his sheep were destroyed by fire; his camels were taken by the Chaldeans; nearly all his servants were slain; and his seven sons killed in a storm (Job 1:13-19). He had been great all time, but a deeper and nobler greatness began to shine like pure gold. He "fell down upon the ground, and worshipped, and said, Naked came I out of my mother's womb, and naked shall I return thither: the Lord gave, and the Lord hath taken away; blessed be the name of the Lord" (Job 1:20,21). "In all

this Job sinned not, nor charged God foolishly" (Job 1:22).

This was not all. He was afflicted "with sore boils from the sole of his foot unto his crown." And there was his wife to contend with, who said, "Dost thou still retain thine integrity? curse God, and die" (Job 2:9). But Job stood the storm. He faithfully replied, "Thou speakest as one of the foolish women speaketh. What? shall we receive good at the hand of God, and shall we not receive evil?" (Job 2:10). There were also friends who chided him, but Job withstood the fiery trials of opposing forces. He said, "When he hath tried me, I shall come forth as gold" (Job 23:10). And he did!

6. *Contrary winds can strengthen us by calling for more fortitude.* God permits things to be fixed against us to teach us to set ourselves against them. We are potential heroes and heroines, but each must prevail in his or her struggle. We are kings and queens in our own little kingdom, but each must battle all the way up to the throne or else be too weak to reign.

Moses had to go through a preparatory period of struggle to ready himself for the great task of leading the children of Israel out of Egyptian bondage.

An easy liver is like a mushroom, which, growing up in a night, is but a pulpy thing. But the oak — ah, there are men who are like this (Psa. 1:1-3). The winds cry, "We will wrestle with you and break you"; and the oak stretches out its limbs and answers, "Let us wrestle, then!" The rocks beneath mutter, "We'll thwart you"; but the oak thrusts down its roots, grapples with the rocks and conquers them. It stands and is stronger than ever, for the storm only sent its roots deeper; while the protected plant in the hothouse is comparatively weak. Thus we wrestle with things which go wrong, opposing forces, and in the wrestling develop those graces, which, bound in a bundle, are called character. Perfection? No! Blunder? Yes, all the way. Beaten? Never! We remain unconquered. We find strength proportionate to the testing. Experience teaches us: "As thy days, so shall thy strength be" (Deut. 33:25).

III. SOME DISTRESSING WINDS WE MUST MEET

1. *Betrayal by supposed friends.* Jesus had this heartbreaking experience. Judas gave him the kiss of betrayal, but Jesus had no animosity. Occasionally we experience a Judas kiss; and when it occurs we need to recall: "The disciple is not above his master, nor the servant above his lord" (Matt. 10:24).

2. *Persecution by enemies.* This is another opportunity for us to be blessed (Matt. 5:11). We cannot control the conduct of others, but we can control our own conduct. We can pray for them. Jesus said, "Pray for them which despitefully use you, and persecute you" (Matt. 5:44).

3. *Lying tongues which hurt you* in church work, in your club, in your business and in your neighborhood. This was one of the sufferings of Jesus. "Where there is smoke there is a little fire" — oh, no, there was a lot of smoke about Jesus, Joseph, Paul and many others, but there was no fire at all. The smoke was only the result of lying tongues, spread by gossipers. This is one of the most annoying experiences — such a foul and unfair way of fighting another — but you can meet it by blessing "them that curse you," by doing "good to them that hate you" (Matt. 5:44). This requires bigness and greatness; and, while we are not as big as we wish, we can keep striving.

4. *Financial backsets* which may be loss of job, failure to get a promotion or an unwise investment. But the world must keep on turning. The Christian does not give up.

If I cannot do what I wish, then I must wish to do what I can. Here is a principle of the Christian's philosophy which helps us to make the adjustment: "A man's life consisteth not in the abundance of the things which he possesseth" (Lk. 12:15). There are advantages in disadvantages.

I know the president of a bank who lost every penny he had during the Great Depression. Did he give up? Not that man. He bought a few used suits and went on foot from place to place selling them. He began to accumulate a little money. Then he opened a used clothing and furniture store. He began to make more money. Then he went into the oil business and became rich again. A former bank president not too proud to walk from house to house selling used clothing — opposing winds did not stop him.

5. *An accident which brings physical and financial injury.* This can teach us patience, and the mastery of self, and thus Paul's words become our words: "I have learned, in whatsoever state I am, therewith to be content" (Phil. 4:11). The reverse can also give impetus to new resolves and again we say in the language of Paul: "Forgetting those things which are behind," I reach "forth unto those things which are before" (Phil. 3:13).

6. *Loss of health.* It may be ourselves or another in the family. In either case, it is a matter of grave concern. In most cases, lost health is regained; if it is not, we can learn to live with the ailment and become stronger spiritually because of the handicap. This was true of Gaius to whom John wrote: "Beloved, I wish above all things that thou mayest prosper and be in health, even as thy soul prospereth" (III Jno. 2). Sickness has brought to many people their highest health. Obstacles can be turned into steppingstones.

If we suffer from an ailment that cannot be cured, then we should accept it gracefully. Self-acceptance will save us from useless resentment over what has happened to us. Victory over adversity can bring our finest days. Paul had a thorn in the flesh (II Cor. 12:7), but at the end of life wrote, "I have fought a good fight" (II Tim. 4:7).

7. *Disappointments of various kinds.* This has always been the common lot of man, including Paul who said, "Wherefore we would have come unto you, even I Paul, once and again; but Satan hindered us" (I Thess. 2:18). But the disappointment did not throw him — he knew this world is not heaven. It is by remaking our plans and renewing our grit that disappointment becomes appointment — and we have been blessed.

8. *Death of a loved one.* This is always a crushing experience. It is God's will that men die, and our world would be unbearable without death. So we can find a balm for bleeding hearts in Job's words: "The Lord gave, and the Lord hath taken away; blessed be the name of the Lord" (Job 1:21). We can also find a stronger impulse and a greater resolve in the language of David: "Wherefore should I fast? can I bring him back again? I shall go to him, but he shall not return to me" (II Sam. 12:23).

IV. FAITH IS SOMETIMES LOST WHEN THINGS GO WELL

1. *There is the danger of losing faith when things go well.* It is this danger from uninterrupted prosperity the Psalmist is referring to when he says, "Because they have no changes, therefore they fear not God" (Psa. 55:19). Certainly, prosperity and untroubled lives have their own searching trials of faith.

2. *One of the disadvantages of good times can be forgetfulness of God.* This was the tragic error of the rich fool in the parable (Lk. 12:16-20). One of the strange per-

versites of human nature is the likelihood to leave God out when the sun is shining, but how quickly we call upon him when the clouds form.

3. Another is pride and self-sufficiency. Uninterrupted prosperity has a tendency to engender these feelings — and they lead to a fall (Prov. 16:18).

V. CONCLUSION

Stormy waves cause the anchor to take a stronger grip. Contrary winds can be instructive, corrective, sanctifying and satisfying. No matter which way the wind blows, I can so set my sails that it shall be to my advantage.

> Then whatsoever wind doth blow,
> My heart is glad to have it so:
> And blow it east or blow it west,
> The wind that blows, that wind is best.
>
> — Caroline A. Mason

REVIEW EXERCISE

1. What special reason was given for the disciples' "toiling in rowing"? ....

2. Why did a woman tell lies on Joseph? ....

3. How does chastening seem at the present? ....

4. What did Job say to his wife when she advised him to curse God and die? ....

5. What did Job say we would receive "at the hand of God"? ....

6. Quote a passage which is helpful to those who suffer financial backsets. ....

7. What was John's wish for Gaius? ....

8. Name fifteen contrary winds given in II Cor. 11:24-27 Paul had to face. ....

9. In making our plans, we should say, "If the Lord ...., we shall ...., and do ...., or ...."

10. Job said that he would come forth as .... when he was tried.

11. Quote a passage which shows that we can find strength proportionate to the testing. ....

12. Paul would have visited the Thessalonians "once and again; but" ....

13. (T or F) David stated that he could not go to his son, but that he would not fast.

14. (T or F) Good times may divert one's interest from God.

15. (T or F) The godly man is compared to a tree by the rivers of water.

16. Thought question: Have you had an experience in life you thought was a contrary wind which actually blew you in the right direction?

XI
The Problem of Self-Imprisonment

I. INTRODUCTION

A FEW years ago a tense, nervous man who figuratively seemed to be wearing a ball and chain came to my office seeking advice. He was frustrated because of inner conflicts. He had fastened the chain of his own making to himself, but now there was a desire to go free. While he was pulling at the chain to break away, he was also struggling with the desire to be bound by it. The battle between self-imprisonment and self-escape raged within him. The result was tattered nerves, crippling inferiority and haunting fear. He said, "I feel like a man in prison seeking freedom."

He was told, "You can be set free, but not without your help. Your thoughts and attitudes imprisoned you; now they must be changed to free you. False feelings about your life (your mistakes, your talents, your relationships with others and your opportunities) must be replaced with true beliefs and true feelings. "And ye shall know the truth, and the truth shall make you free" (Jno. 8:32). For as a man "thinketh in his heart, so is he" (Prov. 23:7).

The apostle Paul once said, "But I was free-born" (Acts 22:28). That can be said of all of us in America, but are we really free? We can build for our occupancy castles of liberty or dungeons of confinement. It seems preposterous that free people would imprison themselves, but millions have. The prison bars we have forged deny us the liberty to seek and find the richer and fuller life of confidence, courage, achievement, success and happiness.

There are many prisons besides the ones made of stone and iron bars. "Stone walls do not a prison make, nor iron bars a cage." There are harder and stronger bars than those made of iron. In the prison of our own thoughts we wear the ball and chain of bondage which languishes personality, wastes talents, locks opportunity and bars success. One of the characters of Charles Dickens expressed it correctly when he said, "I wear the chain I forged in life."

II. PRISON OF INFERIORITY

1. *This is an exaggerated sense of inadequacy.* It fosters a feeling of defeat; and, if permitted to dominate your life, it will defeat and imprison you within the bars of constriction.

2. *All of us at times have to fight the feeling of inferiority.* The self-assertive, forward person is no exception. That bumptious person is more a prisoner of inferiority than the modest one. His acting as though he knows it all is only an effort to bolster his lagging spirits.

3. *The feeling of insufficiency is certainly no proof that one is incapable.* It is a common ailment and, in most instances, without grounds to justify it — just a chain that the person himself has forged. And, oh! how many people are unnecessarily shackled with it.

Preachers ordinarily receive many flowers in their work and a few brickbats. The criticism can be so devastating that if it were not for the flowers one would in time develop an inferiority complex. A preacher friend who was

THE PROBLEM OF SELF-IMPRISONMENT

about ready to break beneath his burdens came into my office a few years ago. When he stepped into the door I could see that he carried with him the atmosphere of gloom, pessimism and defeat. He had the spirit of hopelessness and uselessness written all over his face.

"What is the trouble, Bill?" I asked.

He explained that there was a little opposition to him in the congregation — not over one or two per cent — and that they had in mind another man for his job.

I asked, "How do the elders feel about you?"

He continued: "They are for me — oh! it may be that one is wavering some because of the pressures of that little group. And that is what I wanted to discuss — the elders have asked me to preach this year in our meeting; and I consented, but I don't think I can do it. As I get closer to the starting date, I lose more and more confidence in myself. One of my detractors secretly started the rumor that they needed a bigger preacher for the meeting. You see, if that meeting does not succeed, I'm through there."

I knew he would have to break out of that prison, whether he stayed or went somewhere else. I said, "Bill, you must hold that meeting. You must win that battle you are fighting with inferiority, and you can. You are a capable and effective preacher; I know you are; and the elders know you are. You must prove to yourself that you are more efficient than you have ever been, that you can hold a great meeting for that church. The preacher you mentioned is a worthy and competent man, and I would not say anything disparaging about him; but he is not as capable as you."

He did . . . the meeting was a glorious success.

4. *We can tear down those prison walls of inferiority we have built around ourselves.*

(1) To do so, we cannot submit to them. We have to struggle for everything that is worthwhile and that includes personal freedom. Paul said, "I have fought a good fight" (II Tim. 4:7) — what all that included, we do not know. We do know that Paul had a personal problem, a thorn in the flesh; but he did not give in to it. With God's sufficient grace, he could say, "When I am weak, then am I strong" (II Cor. 12:10).

(2) When we are threatened with the feelings of inferiority we need to take our problem to God in prayer and discuss it with him. It seems that some problems defy solution except on our knees. Nehemiah and his helpers in rebuilding the walls of Jerusalem were the objects of enough ridicule to give anyone an inferiority complex, if that would. These words were hurled at them: "Even that which they build, if a fox go up, he shall even break down their stone wall" (Neh. 4:3). The next verse gives us their reaction — they prayed, and they prayed again.

(3) In the next place, we need to engage in positive thinking, trusting in the Lord to help us. Run these verses through your mind several times each day:

> God is our refuge and strength, a very present help in trouble. — Psa. 46:1

> Unless the Lord had been my help, my soul had almost dwelt in silence. — Psa. 93:17

> I believed, and therefore have I spoken. — II Cor. 4:13

> I can do all things through Christ which strengtheneth me. — Phil. 4:13

There is power in saying, "I can," whatever my difficulty is.

III. PRISON OF SELF-SATISFACTION

1. *Self-satisfaction has become for many people the self-made prison which has restricted their activities.* They are not free to develop their native potentialities and to take advantage of the world's possibilities because they are self-satisfied. Self-satisfaction is a kind of living death — no climbing, growth or improvement. Some people cannot be any better, because they do not want to be any different. This was the underlying fault of the Laodiceans who said, "I am rich, and increased with goods, and have need of nothing" (Rev. 3:17).

2. *Life is a big undertaking and everyone has the privilege and duty of running it in the most efficient way.* As we plan and work to improve our lives, we are called blessed (Matt. 5:3-12). As we grow bigger our opportunities grow bigger. They have been before us all time, but we had to grow a bigger vision before we could see them. Self-satisfied and devoid of vision, we occupy the death cell in our own little prison. "Where there is no vision, the people perish" (Prov. 29:18).

3. *Most people are satisfied if they live up to the standards and demands of the average.* But the Bible admonishes us to excel: "Seek that ye may excel" (I Cor. 14:12). That will put us above the midway mark. There are certain standards of morality, respectability and accomplishment held up by averages, and a person cannot fall below that level and have the approval of society's average. However, those who could have the ambition to excel the average may be pulled down and restrained by the influence of the average. Here is a ball and chain for each ankle: "I am doing as well as the other fellow." "Why should I be expected to do better than the average?"

IV. PRISON OF SUPERSTITION

1. *Many people in the land of the free are held in the bondage of superstition.* Irrational fear of the mysterious keeps them on a short chain in the execution of their duties. When Friday the 13th comes, the world has to stand still for them. They can neither make nor execute a decision on that day; neither can they begin nor end a trip on that date. If a black cat crosses their path, all special activities for that day must be cancelled. If they break a mirror, it is such an omen of trouble that they feel compelled to go to bed to prevent it — they are not free.

2. *Superstition has reached such proportions that the American people are spending over $125,000,000 every year patronizing the various forms of it.* Almost one-half of the American people believe in some form of fortune-telling. Instead of going to the Bible for guidance and comfort (Psa. 119:105), they allow life to be shaped by a certain day, a black cat, a ladder, a broken mirror, or a toothless old lady in a dirty tent. A new kind of pagan society!

3. *We are commanded to remain free of superstition and other fables.* "But refuse profane and old wives' fables, and exercise thyself rather unto godliness" (I Tim. 4:7).

4. *In proportion to our belief in God's running this world, we are freed of superstition.* "God that made the world and all things therein, seeing that he is Lord of heaven and earth" (Acts 17:24). Paul said, "For I know whom I have believed, and am persuaded that he is able to keep that which I have committed unto him against that day" (II Tim. 1:12) — so why should I be made a prisoner by the unfounded fears of superstition? "For in him we live, and move, and have our being" (Acts 17:28) — not in omens and charms.

V. PRISON OF RESTLESSNESS

1. *A generation of bewildered, perplexed people pace* their little prison like a lion in a cage. Just a casual glance at humanity reveals that our society is a restless one. Our people are on the move, but they are not free. They are like caged animals. They are like restless waves of the sea, disquieting their surroundings, with no destiny other than to splash against the shore. Everyday our newspapers scream at us in bold print the message of a troubled world.

Giving themselves to intoxicants is the futile search of a restless people to find release. They are trying to drown their troubles but come nearer drowning themselves. They are searching for peace but in the wrong way. "And be not drunk with wine, wherein is excess; but be filled with the Spirit" (Eph. 5:18).

Gambling is not only a manifestation of materialism, but also of unrest.

Our vision of greener pastures across the fence is oftentimes only an illusion created by our own restlessness. In most cases the grass is green in our own pasture . . . if we would only look.

There are as many as 25,000 suicides some years in America. They try to solve their problems by destroying themselves instead of the things that vex them.

Much of the rushing hither and thither in a world of amusement and pleasure is only a superficial effort to find release for an imprisoned and troubled spirit.

2. *How do we solve this universal problem of unrest?* Here are some suggestions:

(1) We must understand the true design of living. A

false ideal of the ends of living has confused man; so only a true ideal can calm him. Many people think their only purpose for living is to seek pleasure; and the more they search for it, the more they lose it. We are not here just to eat, drink, lust and chase a falling star. Outward experiences can never satisfy the inner longings. Inasmuch as man is spirit as well as flesh, then the restful life necessitates a communion with the Great Spirit. "Let us hear the conclusion of the whole matter: Fear God, and keep his commandments; for this is the whole duty of man" (Eccl. 12:13).

(2) Jesus said, "Come unto me, all ye that labor and are heavy laden, and I will give you rest" (Matt. 11:28). He can bear our burdens. He can give us peace (Phil. 4:7). By giving ourselves to a cause bigger than ourselves, we find something challenging and satisfying for which we live and work . . . and no cause is as big and blessed as the cause of Christ.

(3) Another thing which makes for tranquillity is an approving conscience — "a conscience void of offense toward God, and toward man" (Acts 24:16).

(4) We are more apt to find peace if we quit thinking so much about ourselves and start thinking more about others. It is the person with the big heart, always busy doing for others, who finds happiness. Our Master lived and died for the sake of others — "though he was rich, yet for your sakes he became poor, that ye through his poverty might be rich" (II Cor. 8:9). "For your sakes" — that tells the story of his life — unselfishness; and he lived a calm and serene life in a restless and turbulent world.

One of my daily problems is to remain free of self-imprisonments; and whatever that entails, that is my daily job.

THE PROBLEM OF SELF-IMPRISONMENT

REVIEW EXERCISE

1. Who is our strength? ....
2. Through what power was Paul able to do all things? ....
3. Which parable did the Lord give to teach that he expects each to produce in keeping with his ability? ....
4. What is the conclusion of the whole matter? ....
5. What three words tell the story of Christ's life? ....
6. Which Scripture teaches that man has no more liberty than he thinks? ....
7. What did Paul say he was when he was weak? ....
8. "Seek that ye may ...."
9. "For in him we ...., and ...., and have our ...."
10. We should be filled with the .... rather than .... Scripture: ....
11. Though Christ was .... he became poor for our ....
12. As we plan and work to improve our lives, we are called............
13. (T or F) Paul said, "I have fought a losing fight."
14. (T or F) An approving conscience makes for tranquility.
15. (T or F) There is no rest for those who labor and are heavy laden.
16. Thought question: What are the traits of the person you consider to be the least self-imprisoned of all your acquaintances?

XII
The Problem of Self-Discovery

I. INTRODUCTION

SELF-DISCOVERY is a big and personal problem. Each needs to discover himself. The need is more common than many suppose. Most people seem to have a very imperfect conception of what they really are.

II. SOME WHO FAILED TO SEE THEMSELVES AS THEY WERE

1. *David, one of the all-time greats, marked his life with a failure to see himself as he was.* He, the king, became familiar with a soldier's wife, Bathsheba. She became with child. David ordered the captain to put the soldier-husband, Uriah, in the hottest part of the battle so he would be killed . . . he was. Then David took the woman to be his wife.

The Lord sent Nathan who related this story to David:

> There were two men in one city; the one rich and the other poor.
>
> The rich man had exceeding many flocks and herds:
>
> But the poor man had nothing, save one little ewe lamb, which he had bought and nourished up: and it grew up together with him, and with his children; it did eat of his own meat, and drank of his own cup, and lay in his bosom, and was unto him as a daughter.
>
> And there came a traveler unto the rich man, and he spared to take of his own flock and of his own herd, to dress for the wayfaring man that was come unto him; but

took the poor man's lamb, and dressed it for the man that was come to him.

— II Sam. 12:1-4

"David's anger was greatly kindled against the man; and he said to Nathan, As the Lord liveth, the man that hath done this thing shall surely die: And he shall restore the lamb fourfold, because he did this thing, and because he had no pity" (II Sam. 12:5,6).

"And Nathan said to David, Thou art the man" (II Sam. 12:7).

Then David discovered himself and confessed his sin. He said, "I have sinned against the Lord" (II Sam. 12:13).

The moral for us is: We may have many wonderful and noble traits and still need to discover ourselves.

2. *The Pharisee who went up to the temple to pray did not see his true state* (Lk. 18:10-14). He rather went to brag on himself, for that is what he did in his prayer. He told God how good he was and thanked God he was not like the poor, downcast publican who stood afar off. But the publican had a different view of self. "He would not lift up so much as his eyes unto heaven, but smote his breast, saying, God be merciful to me a sinner." And "this man went down to his house justified rather than the" Pharisee. One saw himself as he was, while the other did not.

3. *The members of the church at Laodicea had a grossly perverted view of themselves* (Rev. 3:14-17). Here is their self-appraisal: "Thou sayest, I am rich, and increased with goods, and have need of nothing." But the Lord told them the truth about themselves. We may fool ourselves, but not the Lord.

III. SOME WHO DISCOVERED THEMSELVES

1. *The chief butler, made famous by Joseph and Joseph's*

dreams, saw his faulty life. He said to Pharaoh, "I do remember my faults this day" (Gen. 41:9).

John stated that a failure to recognize sin in our lives is self-deception: "If we say that we have no sin, we deceive ourselves, and the truth is not in us" (I Jno. 1:9).

2. *Isaiah got a more vivid and realistic picture of self when he saw his sinful nature in contrast with God's holy nature.* Isaiah's appraisal of self was too high until he saw the glory of God, and then he exclaimed: "Woe is me! for I am undone, because I am a man of unclean lips" (Isa. 6:5). Undone! And we shall never be done as long as we live in the flesh. Paul said, "Brethren, I count not myself to have apprehended . . . I press toward the mark for the prize of the high calling of God in Christ Jesus" (Phil. 3:13,14).

3. *Peter found himself out in the most painful way.* He sincerely thought he was beyond denial of Christ. Peter said, "Though all men shall be offended because of thee, yet will I never be offended" (Matt. 26:33). Jesus said unto him, Verily I say unto thee, That this night, before the cock crow, thou shalt deny me thrice" (Matt. 26:34). But Peter had a higher opinion of himself than this and assured himself with these words, "Though I should die with thee, yet will I not deny thee" (Matt. 26:35). But he did! And when the cock crew, he remembered the word of Jesus and "went out, and wept bitterly."

Peter was well warned by Christ of the weakness within him; but he would not believe it until he went on to find out for himself through base denial, falsehood and cursing, the enormous possibilities of waywardness that dwelt within him.

When we think we are too strong to fall, we may drop

our guard and prove ourselves too weak to stand. The Bible says, "Wherefore let him that thinketh he standeth take heed lest he fall" (I Cor. 10:12).

4. *The prodigal son* — "And when he came to himself" (Lk. 15:17); that is, when he saw himself as he was, his frailties and perverseness on the one hand and his better self and nobility on the other. The prodigal son had not only lost sight of his father and his family and his home, but he had lost sight of himself. He had lost sight of reason, his better nature and all that constituted him a man. When his money was wasted, his capacity blunted and his character gone, then the reaction came. While he wanted food for the body, there was a more ravenous hunger of the heart. There was the pigs' slop for his stomach, but no sustenance for his heart. His low physical state plus his yearning for sympathy, respect and love brought him to his senses. He "came to himself," made a real self-discovery. Self-knowledge opened his eyes to himself — this was his first victory in his subsequent program of self-improvement.

His fancy picture of himself was that of a capable, enterprising, independent young man who could manage his own affairs successfully and make his mark in the world, if only he were freed from the chains of the old home. When given the chance to find out, plus his share of the inheritance, lo! heaven help! the excellent gentleman turned out a vile sinner; the capable young man, a pauper; and the independent boy who thought the world could be taken just for the asking, a starving, enslaved feeder of swine. It was then that he came to see himself as he was, made a real self-discovery and knew who he was and what he had done. Experience was a costly teacher, but he learned his lesson.

IV. SELF-DECEPTION

The Bible says, "The heart is deceitful above all things, and desperately wicked: who can know it?" (Jer. 17:9). One of its deceits is to hide its own deceit and thus prevent a man from discovering himself. Deception is a very old practice and is prevalent everywhere; therefore, we want to show some of the ways we deceive ourselves and thus fail to discover our real selves.

1. *One of the most common methods of becoming dupes is the comfortable practice of looking at the sins of others instead of our own.*

There was an elderly man who often wore a coat patched with many colors. He said the patches on the sides represented the sins of his neighbors. When asked about the patches on the back, he replied, "They represent my sins, but they are where I can't see them."

It is easy to see the faults of others, but we seldom see our own. For instance, the spendthrifts can give us a great homily on the sins of the miser; and the miser can preach a sermon equally as strong on the sins of the spendthrift. What deception! What weakness! It is amazing how quick we are to see the mote in other people's eyes and never see the beam in our own eyes. Jesus had something to say on this topic in Matt. 7:3-5.

2. *Another deceitful exercise which hinders self-discovery is the measurement of ourselves by others who are weaker and less fortunate.* We say, "I wouldn't do what he has done. I am better than she is." These comparisons are not wise: "For we dare not make ourselves of the number, or compare ourselves with some that commend themselves: but they, measuring themselves by themselves, and comparing themselves among themselves, are not wise"

(II Cor. 10:12). You see, we can't discover self, if we spend all our time trying to cover self with a false standard. No matter how strong or weak, good or bad the other fellow may be, it does not alter my status one bit. I am what I am, no matter what others are.

Here is the true measurement which enables us to see ourselves as we really are: "But let every man prove his own work, aand then shall he have rejoicing in himself alone, and not in another" (Gal. 6:4). One of my daily problems is to prove or test myself by the true standard of Christ and his word; and if I am true according to this ascertainment, then I can rejoice in myself and not in the weaknesses of another. This is the gauge which gives me my real dimensions, the mirror which reflects my true image. And the feelings I have toward myself are more consequential than those of any human being, provided they are true.

> Just go to the mirror and look at yourself
> And see what that man has to say;
> For it isn't your father, or mother, or wife,
> Who judgment upon you must pass.
> The fellow whose verdict counts most in your life
> Is the one staring back from the glass.
> — Author unknown

3. *We are hindered from self-discovery by assuming virtues which are not our own.* Here is a man who takes pride in his family, but what has he done to make his family name great and honorable? Here is another man who prides himself upon belonging to a large, active and generous church, but what has he done? That's the question.

It is a matter of self-deception. A man is not honorable because he has an upright family; neither is he an active and generous Christian just because he has membership in a live and liberal congregation.

What I need to do is examine myself and see if I have the virtues I am proud to recognize in the group to which I belong. "But let a man examine himself, and so let him eat of that bread, and drink of that cup" (I Cor. 11:28). "Examine yourselves, whether ye be in the faith; prove your own selves" (II Cor. 13:5).

4. We deceive ourselves by disguising our sins with new names. That is the way we try to make them look good. You have seen the covetous man who labeled his sin "thrift." And you have seen the stingy man who refused to give to the church who called it humility — he was too humble to let anyone see him give more than a nominal sum. Also, there is the person who neglects worship on the Lord's day, but deceitfully boasts that he or she is a Christian every day in the week — but how could that be if a person neglects God's commands on one day of the week, the Lord's day (Acts 20:7; I Cor. 16:2)?

God has said, "Woe unto them that call evil good, and good evil; that put darkness for light and light for darkness; and put bitter for sweet, and sweet for bitter!" (Isa. 5:20).

5. Self-discovery is hampered by the gratifying deceit of changing the form of our sins. We think that sin is made up in the form in which it is visualized; therefore, we think that by changing the form we have escaped the sin. No! Not in the least! Man reads, "Thou shalt not kill" (Ex. 20:13). And he says, "Thank God, I am not a killer!" while in his heart he may hate an enemy and wish that an automobile would run over him or something else would blot him out of his path. The Bible says, whether we admit it to ourselves or not, "Whosoever hateth his brother is a murderer: and ye know that no murderer hath eternal life abiding in him" (I Jno. 3:15). And one says, "Thank the Lord, I am not a thief!" Nevertheless, he may hold up others for services and goods, if he can. Thus robbery takes on a less dangerous form, so far as this life is concerned. But God said, "Rob not the poor, because he is poor: neither oppress the afflicted in the gate" (Prov. 22:22). And there is the matter of adultery. One thanks God that he is not an adulterer, while he has lust in his heart toward a woman. According to Christ, he is an adulterer, though he has not committed the overt act (Matt. 5:28).

V. CONCLUSION

1. I should diligently and conscientiously strive to discover myself; because, whether I really see myself or not, I tell on myself. I show my faith (and myself too) by my works (Jas. 2:18).

2. Furthermore, I should be honest with myself and try to see myself as I am; because *what I am and what I sow will be my destiny.* "Be not deceived; God is not mocked: for whatsoever a man soweth, that shall he also reap"; sow to the flesh, reap corruption; sow to the Spirit, reap life everlasting (Gal. 6:7,8).

> The tissue of the life to be,
> We weave with colors all our own;
> And on the fields of destiny,
> We reap as we have sown.

3. The time for self-examination is very short. We may masquerade today with a mask; but death will soon strip us, and we must stand before the great Judge after death has discovered us in all our nakedness. So the wise thing is for us to discover ourselves now while time favors us with opportunities to make improvement.

THE CHRISTIAN'S EVERYDAY PROBLEMS

REVIEW EXERCISE

1. What did David say when he discovered himself? ....
2. What was the difference between the Pharisee and the publican who went to the temple to pray? ....
3. What did the chief butler say concerning his faults? ....
   ....
4. What perverted view of themselves did the members of the church at Laodicea hold? ....
   ....
5. What did Jesus say in Matthew 7:3-5 relative to self-deception?
   ....
   ....
   ....
6. What is deceitful above all things? ....
7. Isaiah exclaimed, "Woe is me! for I am ...., because I am a man of ....". Scripture:
   ....
8. .... wept at the crowing of a cock.
9. "And when he came to himself" refers to ....
10. "Woe unto them that call .... good, and .... evil."
11. Quote Peter's statement which shows that he thought he was beyond denial of Christ. ....
    ....
12. Comment: We may fool ourselves, but not the Lord. ....
    ....
    ....

13. (T or F) David ordered the husband of a woman he loved to be put in the hottest part of the battle so he would be killed.
14. (T or F) The Bible says it is helpful to compare ourselves among ourselves.
15. (T or F) Man tells on himself by his works.

XIII
The Problem of Self-Improvement

I. INTRODUCTION

WE have the daily challenge to improve ourselves and to develop more beautiful and beneficient lives. God's plan for the Christian is a life of betterment, as seen in the following Scriptures:

"Therefore leaving the principles of the doctrine of Christ, let us go on unto perfection" (Heb. 6:1).

"Wherefore laying aside all malice, and all guile, and hypocrisies, and envies, and all evil speakings, as newborn babes, desire the sincere milk of the word, that ye may grow thereby" (I Pet. 2:1,2).

Each of the above-quoted Scriptures calls for a conscious effort of self-improvement. Only by becoming a better person can I meet with God's approval. Few things remain static, including the development of character. So I must pull myself up through purposeful and conscious efforts or aimlessly allow myself to be pulled down by the cares and forces surrounding me. I have a daily problem, but it is also my daily opportunity to enrich my character and ennoble my life.

II. WAYS AND MEANS OF SELF-IMPROVEMENT

Here are some definite and sure suggestions for the enlargement and expansion of the likable and lovable life:

THE PROBLEM OF SELF-IMPROVEMENT

1. *Self-discovery is a prerequisite to self-improvement.* This was discussed in the previous chapter.

2. *Reading the Bible everyday encourages personal excellence.*

(1) The most revealing agency in self-discovery — essential to self-improvement — is God's word, which is described as a mirror for the soul (Jas. 1:23-25). As we conscientiously look into the Bible, we see a reflection of all our moral and spiritual blotches and disfigurements which need attention and correction.

(2) The Bible is a sword which cuts and pricks the heart, and all self-amendment begins with the heart; "for out of it are the issues of life" (Prov. 4:23). "For the word of God is quick, and powerful, and sharper than any two-edged sword, piercing even to the dividing asunder of soul and spirit, and of the joints and marrow, and is a discerner of the thoughts and intents of the heart" (Heb. 4:12). It will cut. It will prick. It will discern our thoughts and intents. In speaking of the people on Pentecost who heard God's word, we read, "Now when they heard this, they were pricked in their heart" (Acts 2:37). Changes followed, but they were effected by the cutting power of God's word. The Sword of the Spirit will cut the heart and change our thinking; and as our thinking improves, our lives are refined and beautified. We are imperfect enough reading the Bible — how much worse we would be without it!

(3) The Bible is like a fire and a hammer, which burns up the dross and pulverizes the hardness of the heart. "Is not my word like as a fire? saith the Lord; and like a hammer that breaketh the rock in pieces?" (Jer. 23:29). If we want the dross consumed and the heart refined, read

the Bible. If we want the heart softened and tendered, read the Bible.

(4) God's word is a nourishment which produces growth. It is called "milk" (I Pet. 2:2) and "strong meat" (Heb. 5:12). As mentioned in I Peter 2:1, it gives us strength to outgrow "all malice, and all guile, and hypocrisies, and envies, and all evil speakings." And the Lord knows most people are still in need of maturing out of some, if not all, of these personality-destroying, soul-shrinking traits.

(5) The word of God furnishes man unto every good work (II Tim. 3:16,17). If I would adorn my life, I need to engage in good works; and the Bible tells me what they are and inspires me to do them.

Yes, there is productive and revitalizing power in that Book. By reading and meditating on it everyday — not just once a week — we contact an elevating power which has always been an influence for good, a blessed experience (Psa. 1:1-3).

I knew a lovely, elderly woman who said that she had read the Bible through fourteen times, and each time for the specific purpose of seeing if there was anything God had commanded her to do that she was not doing. She was blessed.

Great men have lifted high the praises of the Bible and focused attention on its merits:

> Every hour I read you, it kills a sin or lets a virtue in to fight it.
> — Isaac Walton

> It is impossible to mentally or socially enslave a Bible-reading people.
> — Horace Greeley

> We are indebted to the Book of books for cur ideals

and institutions. Their preservation rests in adhering to its principles. The study of the Bible is a rich post-graduate course in the richest library of human experience.

— Herbert Hoover

It is impossible rightly to govern the world without God and the Bible.

— George Washington

There is no solid basis for civilization but in the Word of God. I make it a practice to read the Bible through once every year.

— Daniel Webster

The Psalmist said, "Thy word have I hid in mine heart, that I might not sin against thee" (Psa. 119:11).

3. *We can upgrade our lives by picking associates who contribute to our goodness.* Here is a warning: "Be not deceived: evil communications [companionships, A.S.V.] corrupt good manners [morals, A.S.V.]" (I Cor. 15:33). Associations are like leaven; and "Know ye not that a little leaven leaveneth the whole lump?" (I Cor. 5:6). If we run with goats, we are going to smell like them. If we want to be a "sweet savor" of life (II Cor. 2:15), we must watch our companionships.

God issued this protective command: "Make no friendship with an angry man; and with a furious man thou shalt not go" — why? — "lest thou learn his ways, and get a snare to thy soul" (Prov. 22:24,25). "Learn his ways" — that's what we do. "His ways" may be a snare or a savor. Thus I should be cautious, for "his ways" may become my ways.

The ways of Solomon's wives became his ways — "his wives turned away his heart after other gods" (I Ki. 11:4). He was a wise man, but not wise enough.

The ways of Herod's guests were adopted as his ways — "for the oath's sake, and them which sat with him at meat, he ... beheaded John" (Matt. 14:9,10). Herod dined with the wrong crowd.

The ways of a Christian wife may be transferred through the power of influence to an alien husband and thus lead to his conversion — "if any obey not the word, they also may without the word be won by the conversation [behavior, A.S.V.] of the wives" (I Pet. 3:1). He may keep a closed Bible, but his wife's life is an open gospel he cannot help but read — a fifth gospel which influences lives.

> You are writing a gospel, a chapter a day,
> By deeds that you do, and by words that you say;
> Men read what you write whether faithless or true —
> Say, what is the gospel according to you?

4. *We can cultivate the more attractive personality by thinking on the right things.* Man is the accumulation of his thoughts. Solomon said, "For as he thinketh in his heart, so is he" (Prov. 23:7). Beautiful deeds are the outward manifestations of an inward beauty. We have heard it said: "Pretty is as pretty does"; and we can further say, "If pretty does, it is because pretty is on the inside." We may beautify ourselves on the inside — and consequently in deeds — by controlling our thinking. The best way to control evil thinking is to be busy and absorbed in righteous thinking. God is the author of the plan of positive, righteous thinking. He has said, "Finally, brethren, whatsoever things are true, whatsoever things are honest, whatsoever things are just, whatsoever things are pure, whatsoever things are lovely, whatsoever things are of good report; if there be any virtue, and if there be any praise, think on these things" (Phil. 4:8). This is so much more elevating and ennobling than thinking on things

false, dishonest, unjust, impure, ugly, censorious, immoral and of evil report. No one should allow his heart to become a garbage can for society's filth.

5. *Examination of one's daily life with the resolution to excel is a stimulus to better living.* There should be a concerted, honest, systematic effort. There should be a thoughtful, definite plan rather than a thoughtless, haphazard procedure. For instance, it would be helpful to have a chart listing the areas where we wish to make improvement and each night review the chart and grade ourselves for that day. Here are some fields of human thought and endeavor in which we should question ourselves:

(1) Have I spoken evil of any person this day? "Speak not evil one of another, brethren" (Jas. 4:11).

(2) Have I taken the name of God in vain? "Thou shalt not take the name of the Lord thy God in vain" (Ex. 20:7).

(3) Have I been a gossiper? "Thou shalt not go up and down as a talebearer among thy people" (Lev. 19:16).

(4) Have I this day been quick to speak and quick to wrath? "Let every man be swift to hear, slow to speak, slow to wrath" (Jas. 1:19).

(5) Have I been a peacemaker on the job, in the school, in the church and in every walk of life? "Let us therefore follow after the things which make for peace" (Rom. 14:19).

(6) Have I been unselfish in all my dealings? "Look not every man on his own things, but every man also on the things of others" (Phil. 2:4).

(7) Have I this day been free of malice and hate? "For we ourselves also were sometimes foolish, disobedient, deceived, serving divers lusts and pleasures, living in malice

and envy, hateful, and hating one another" (Tit. 3:3).

(8) Have I been free of envy of another's honor, position, possessions or success? "But envy is the rottenness of the bones" (Prov. 14:30).

(9) Have I been compassionate and sympathetic? "Finally, be ye all of one mind, having compassion one of another; love as brethren, be pitiful, be courteous" (I Pet. 3:8).

(10) Have I refrained from being retaliatory and vengeful? "Not rendering evil for veil, or railing for railing: but contrariwise blessing" (I Pet. 3:9).

(11) Have I been longsuffering and gentle? "But the fruit of the Spirit is love, joy, peace, long-suffering, gentleness, goodness, faith" (Gal. 5:22).

(12) Have I this day been sincere in all my affairs? "That ye may be sincere and without offense till the day of Christ" (Phil. 1:10).

(13) Have I been honest in all my dealings? "Thou shalt not steal" (Ex. 20:15).

(14) Have I been cooperative in the home, on the job, and in the church? "We then as workers together" (II Cor. 6:1).

(15) Have I been tolerant of the faults of others, considering myself? "And why beholdest thou the mote that is in thy brother's eye, but considerest not the beam that is in thine own eye?" (Matt. 7:3).

(16) Have I been fair and just in all my relationships? "What doth the Lord require of thee, but to do justly, and to love mercy, and to walk humbly with thy God?" (Mic. 6:8).

(17) Have I been forgiving, refusing to harbor grudges? "But if ye forgive not men their trespasses, neither will your Father forgive your trespasses" (Matt. 6:15).

(18) Have I been thankful for my blessings? "Be ye thankful" (Col. 3:15).

(19) Have I been industrious? "Slothfulness casteth into a deep sleep; and an idle soul shall suffer hunger" (Prov. 19:15).

(20) Have I been thrifty? "Gather up the fragments that remain, that nothing be lost" (Jno. 6:12).

(21) Have I kept my word? "Covenant-breakers . . . worthy of death" (Rom. 1:21,32).

(22) Have I been easy to entreat? "But the wisdom that is from above is first pure, then peaceable, gentle, and easy to be entreated" (Jas. 3:17).

(23) Have I today followed the Golden Rule? "Therefore all things whatsoever ye would that men should do to you, do ye even so to them" (Matt. 7:12).

(24) Have I been content in the path that I must travel? "For I have learned in whatsoever state I am, therewith to be content" (Phil. 4:11).

(25) Have I today found happiness and shared it with others? "Rejoice in the Lord always: and again I say: Rejoice" (Phil. 4:4).

This list can be modified, increased or decreased, to suit the individual's own personal needs for self-improvement. The list should be checked nightly, giving yourself a grade, with the determination to make a better score tomorrow.

There is much power in resolution. There is dormant

energy in saying, "I can." There is motivating power in saying, "I will."

I WILL

I will start afresh each new day from petty littleness freed;
I will cease to stand complaining of my ruthless neighbor's greed;
I will try to find contentment in the paths that I must tread;
I will never have resentment when another gets ahead.
I will open my eyes to beauty before me, rain or shine;
I will not meddle with your life, but apply myself to improving mine.

We are human and that means imperfect; so we shall never be perfect in this life, but we can have a perfect goal. Browning said, "Oh! but a man's reach should exceed his grasp." We are faulty enough without having an inferior and and a defective goal; therefore, "let us go on unto perfection" (Heb. 6:1).

REVIEW EXERCISE

1. What did Peter say newborn babes should lay aside? ....

2. What is the mirror that reveals our true self? ....

3. What is the discerner of the thoughts and intents of the heart?

4. What are the words which describe the nourishing qualities of God's word? ....

5. Why did the Psalmist hide God's word in his heart? ....

6. Why are we commanded not to make a friendship with an angry man? ....

7. What tribute did Peter pay to the influence of godly wives?

THE PROBLEM OF SELF-IMPROVEMENT

8. We can cultivate the more attractive personality by thinking upon
   ....
   ....

9. "Let us go on unto ...."

10. If we want the dross consumed and the heart refined, we............
    ....

11. "A little leaven .... the ...."

12. Solomon's "............................... turned away his heart after other
    ...."

13. (T or F) Herod's associates influenced him in the wrong way.

14. (T or F) It is not necessary that we be easily entreated.

15. (T or F) Paul said, "I have learned."

16. Thought question: What good do I receive from asking myself the twenty-five questions given in the chapter?